Copyright © 2021 by Holger Selling IV

All rights reserved. No part of this publication may be reproduced, distributed, or transmitted in any form or by any means, including photocopying, recording, or other electronic or mechanical methods, without the prior written permission of the publisher, except in the case of brief quotations embodied in critical reviews and certain other noncommercial uses permitted by copyright law. For permission requests, write to the publisher, addressed "Attention: Permissions Coordinator," at the address below.

Alpha Book Publisher
www.alphapublisher.com
ISBN: 978-1-954297-49-4

Ordering Information:
Quantity sales. Special discounts are available on quantity purchases by corporations, associations, and others. For details, contact the publisher at the address above.
Orders by U.S. trade bookstores and wholesalers. Visit www.alphapublisher.com/contact-us to learn more.

Printed in the United States of America

Table of Contents

Chapter 1 HOW 1
Chapter 2 Just the Beginning 12
Chapter 3 Progress 18
Chapter 4 Waiting 24
Chapter 5 Turning A Corner 32
Chapter 6 Everything Changed 35
Chapter 7 ECMO 40
Chapter 8 Is It Working? 43
Chapter 9 The Babies 45
Chapter 10 The Long Road Ahead 47
Chapter 11 More Waiting 50
Chapter 12 Business 53
Chapter 13 Turning A Corner 56
Chapter 14 Almost There 60
Chapter 15 Let's Go 64
Chapter 16 Two Steps Forward,
Three Steps Back 72
Chapter 17 Time to Heal 76
Chapter 18 The New Normal 81
Chapter 19 Home 88
Chapter 20 Day to Day 92
Chapter 21 It's Time 100
Chapter 22 How It Came to Be 103

57 Days

How

Chapter 1

There is no rulebook in life. No one prepares you for the unknown. When traumatic events happen, there is no forewarning, it's sink or swim time, and you have two choices, you can bury your head in the sand and let the world swallow you whole, or you can take the bull by the horns and take it head-on. It's been three months since my world was turned upside down, I can reflect on this now that it has passed and really say.

"What the hell!"

But at the time I was thrust into it, I was not asking that. For me it was just time and little did I know my entire world would change in a matter of 57 days.

I am 46 years old. I was born and raised in the Central Valley of California; I own successful businesses here in the Valley. I have three beautiful children and a happy, healthy marriage. Don't get me wrong. My life isn't perfect. Things haven't always been easy. I went through a divorce after being married for 17 years, and I was not looking to join the dating scene. I had two young impressionable boys to raise. I had work and my friends, so I was content. I've never been the guy to be single, I liked having a partner, but I wasn't actively looking for someone. I needed to focus on my kids and myself and just enjoy life. I had met Dallas years before, Clovis is a small town and we had come across each other a handful of times. She was also recently divorced, and we cultivated a friendship. We were very similar. A lot of people thought maybe we were too similar to be a couple, we are both driven, headstrong, and successful people. We both like to keep busy and go…go…go.... We realized pretty quickly that we wanted to be more than just friends. In July of 2017 we got married in an intimate ceremony with family and friends in attendance. Not too long after in 2018 we welcomed our first child together, a daughter we named Utley Davis.

    2020 started much like every other year. I work hard, I enjoy life, and I do my best. COVID-19 had just started to spread here in California. It was all over the news and to be honest I thought this was another cold or flu that has been blown drastically out of proportion. I did not know anyone close to me that had been affected by it, and I was not overly concerned about it. I was cautious but not over the top. I was not about to let sickness slow me down. I couldn't afford that. Halfway through 2020, my wife Dallas and I decided to add to our family and started the process of having another baby. There is a considerable age difference between my two older boys and Utley, and we thought it would be nice for Utley to have a brother or sister. My son Hogi is twenty-one, and Evan is seventeen. Utley is only two. She adores her older brothers. Having more children was something I always wanted, so when my wife told me she was pregnant with baby number 4, I was thrilled, followed by shock when she said we were also having baby number 5. We were having twins. At 16 weeks we had an ultrasound and the doctor let us know it was 2 little girls. I was ecstatic, life was about to change for me in a huge way. Most men would be nervous, or even hesitant, at 46 years old I was bringing two more babies into the world, I would be a father to five children and it was a lot to digest, but after the initial surprise wore off, I was just excited about the whole thing, being a father is second nature to me, I adore my children, so the fact that I was adding two more to my brood didn't faze me, I was ready.

Even with COVID-19 and the state shutting down, everything was seemingly normal for us. We make the best of what we have. My wife and I both have demanding careers, she is a Family Law attorney with her own practice, and I run multiple businesses, the main one being an electrical contracting company with over one hundred employees. We have help, we have an in-home nanny who comes four days a week to help with Utley while Dallas and I are at work. We reserve Fridays as a family day, Dallas stays home, and I try to work a half day. We own a small ranch in Clovis, it sits on 2 acres, and we have horses, goats, dogs, cats and donkeys, so besides work and kids there is never a dull moment, and I wouldn't have it any other way, keeping busy is what I do, I like being busy.

Before I knew it, time had passed, and Dallas was 19 weeks pregnant with our twins.

November has arrived, and we are gearing up for Thanksgiving. The holidays are always a big deal at my house. We always have a full house, my family, her family, lots of friends and their families.

This year Thanksgiving was on Thursday the 26th, and we already had planned a little smaller affair for 2020. With all the COVID restrictions and Dallas being pregnant with twins we did not want to overdo it, so a few family members and some close friends were invited, and we were ready for the day.

Around the same week of Thanksgiving Dallas started to feel sick, she came down with what we thought was a bad cold. She was congested, had a headache, body aches and a bit of a fever. She was really feeling under the weather, pregnant with twins, and already exhausted. We all just thought it may be a cold that would take a little longer to kick. Carrying twins is no easy feat in itself, but she just wasn't getting better, so we decided to get her tested for COVID, her symptoms were conducive with both COVID symptoms and a bad cold/flu, so we did not want to take any chances. We had her take the rapid test, and sure enough, it came back positive for COVID. This diagnosis explained a lot. Her shortness of breath, chest pain, the lingering cough and fever.

I have heard of many people who have had COVID, and their worst symptom was fever and body aches, and the occasional loss of taste and smell, but they recovered and were fine. We were lucky in that respect; it had not hit anyone close to us in any detrimental way. So, we thought, "OK' get her some rest, some meds safe for the babies, and she will be good to go in a matter of days.

Now in hindsight I never thought it was going to be bad, I never thought.

"Oh man, she is going to be hit hard with this."

The thought that I could lose my wife and children never once entered my mind. It honestly didn't. Even now after all is said and done and I sit here and write this book and reflect on everything, I never ever wrapped my head around the thought that I could lose everything. What I thought was this is a bump in the road and she will be fine. Dallas has always been healthy, she eats right, works out, does not smoke, she is in great shape. I thought this would pass. She will be fine, and if anything, she may be sick for a few days, nothing we can't handle.

I'm not that guy, I don't worry unnecessarily, never have been. I don't automatically think the worst. I take the facts, and I work with them. I try to see the positive in every situation. The fact was, she had COVID, and we needed to make sure she got through it. I watch the news so I know it can be bad. But I also know the demographic that was hit the hardest with this pandemic were the elderly or those who had an underlying condition, this was not Dallas. I wasn't hyper-focused on who she got it from, it wouldn't change anything, could have been anyone really.

The way this illness is spreading you just need to touch something or someone who is infected. She has it, and we need to figure out how to keep her healthy. She is carrying not one but two of my children and we need to ensure she gets well, not just for her safety but for my unborn girls as well.

Dallas and I are around people all day, every day. She practices law so she has hearings and meetings all day every day. She was needed and she wasn't going to stop helping people just because people were getting sick. We couldn't stay home; our jobs did not permit that. COVID wasn't going to slow us down. Dallas needed to keep going for her clients. She represents families that needed her.

My business is considered essential, so neither of us stopped working since COVID started, we weren't exposed to it, so we kept going. My employees were glad they needed to work, we were cautious, wearing masks, social distancing and keeping sanitizer on hand at all jobs and in the office. I have hundreds of people who depend on me daily, not just my own family, I am responsible for so many others, closing our doors was not going to happen.

We were both careful, we mask in public, we wash our hands, we don't go out unnecessarily, we go to work, and we take care of our family. We take the necessary precautions, and we keep our circle small.

After Dallas was diagnosed with COVID we continued the motions of having Thanksgiving.

Dallas was not getting better, but she still wanted it to happen. At this point she was still coughing and had a low-grade fever, but she was determined to have Thanksgiving for the kids and I. We had told our friends that were coming over that we had to cancel. We certainly didn't want to expose anyone unnecessarily, so it was just us. Dallas rested most of the day and I tended to the cooking and keeping everyone in the spirit of the holiday. It was quiet but we made the best out of it. We were together and that is all that matters.

     Since Dallas tested positive, we decided to have the kids tested, we needed to be safe, no one else in the family had any symptoms but we are all in such close contact it was the right thing to do. I never got tested, I know there were conversations about this on why I didn't get tested. I am sure it was a conversation amongst friends and family at some point. However, I didn't feel the need, I had no symptoms and I felt fine. Even if I did get tested and it was positive nothing would change, my life does not afford me the luxury of taking two weeks off and taking it easy. Plus, I had to take care of the family now, Dallas was down, and it was all on me. All the things that she usually does, Getting Utley ready for school, getting breakfast ready for us, grocery shopping, it all fell to me now. So, no I didn't get tested and I focused everything I had on her. We hoped with rest and me taking care of everything, that she would get better. We tried all the usual remedies, humidifiers, air purifiers and inhalers, you name it. We had to be careful due to the fact that she is pregnant with twins. However, nothing was working, she was getting worse. We would stay up all night, she was coughing and short of breath, and all together miserable, so neither she nor I was getting any sleep.

    My days here started by getting my daughter up and ready in the morning. I would get her breakfast, brush her hair, brush her teeth and get her dressed. My nanny would arrive and I would make sure Dallas was ok, before I headed out to work. Every hour I would go back home to check in and make sure Dallas was ok or if she needed anything. Not much I could do but check on her. Luckily, my office is only a quick five minutes from my house. Our nanny kept Utley busy while Dallas would try to get some sleep. However, it has been over a week now, and I was feeling hopeless. It was a helpless feeling; she wasn't improving, she sounded worse and she was so run down. I don't know what to do for her. All I can do is make sure she is comfortable and be there for her and my kids and try to take the burden of everything else off her. Luckily, I was not getting sick, I was able to take over all the responsibilities that Dallas usually handled, the house, the kids, and the ranch, all while running my business and making sure she was ok. It was a lot, but I had to get it done. She was depending on me.

    On Nov.29th, I went to work as usual and after a few hours I came home to check on her. I noticed immediately her coloring, she was turning blue and trying to catch her breath after each cough. There was no time to think, I had to get her help. I called 911, and I told them what was going on and that I needed an ambulance. My younger son Evan stood outside our gate to wait for the ambulance while I sat with Dallas and tried to keep her calm. We got her in the ambulance, they started oxygen immediately and drove her to Clovis Community Hospital which is only a few blocks from our home. I followed behind in my own vehicle. There was a makeshift COVID tent outside of the emergency room, and that is where they took her. I could not go in, no one was allowed in, so I waited patiently in my vehicle. The nurses all told her to text me to head home because I would not be coming in. I didn't feel right about leaving, but I had Utley at home with my boys. So, I responded to Dallas and told her to call me, if she needs anything and that I would wait at home for her call.

    I drove home, made my kids dinner, gave Utley a bath and put her to bed and waited by the phone. I was tense, just waiting. I have no one to contact and speak with. She's tired and having tests run, so she can't fill me in. She doesn't even know what's going on. I call the hospital and get transferred a million times before I get the right area to where she is and they tell me the same thing, they are running tests, they don't know yet and they will call me when they have something to tell me. Long hours later I get the call from Dallas to come and get her, there is nothing they can do, she is not sick enough and only 19 weeks pregnant. I'm informed that had she been 20 weeks pregnant, they would have admitted her, but she was only 19 weeks so she could go home. So, at 10 pm I bundled up my sleeping two-year-old and went and picked up my wife.

So now what? I have a sick, pregnant wife who cannot breathe, can't sleep, won't stop coughing, and is all around miserable, but because of the influx of very ill COVID patients and limited room in the hospital, she did not fit the criteria to be admitted. Apparently to them, she isn't that bad. How is this even possible? She is suffering and seriously sick and pregnant with twins. I don't even know what tests they ran. Did they do an X-ray on her? Blood tests? Ct scans? Are the babies ok? Did they do an ultrasound to check. Dallas is exhausted and just wants to sleep. Once again, I am helpless, and I don't know anything, except that in the hospital's eyes she was not sick enough to keep.

I am trying not to worry for her sake because I do not want her to be scared. But by the following day I'm acutely aware that they made a mistake, and this is too much for her. She cannot catch her breath and her breathing in general is extremely labored. I am livid that the hospital sent her home. How can they not see that she is seriously ill, and something needs to be done? It's not just her, it's my two girls she is carrying. If she can't breathe, how am I to know how my babies are doing? Are they still thriving? Is Dallas's lack of oxygen affecting them? It's too soon in her pregnancy and I can't sit idle and watch this happen. So, again I called 911 and asked for the ambulance to take her back. This time it is different, this time they will be keeping her, and I am making sure of it. I called the Head of the hospital foundation to ensure she gets admitted to the hospital. I am pulling out all the cards, and I do not care what anyone thinks, money talks and I write endless checks to this hospital every year and if I need to use that to enforce her stay, then that's what I will do. This time there is no way around it. On Dec.2nd 2020, she was admitted to Community Regional Medical Center. I didn't know then, that this was the 10th day of the hardest 57 days of my life.

Just the Beginning
Chapter 2

I can't sleep. How can I? I don't even know what's going on. I pace, I clean anything and everything to keep me occupied so I don't drive up to the hospital and insist they let me in. I call the hospital and am being told she is getting breathing treatments and she is tired. Very limited information is given to me. She texts me and gives me the info she knows but it is also limited, they are running tests and trying to figure out what is wrong with her. Meanwhile all I can think about is her.

People are aware that my wife is in the hospital, so the texts and calls are streaming in. Her friends, my friends, our family, everyone is concerned. They want to know what is happening, but I just do not have the bandwidth in me right now to deal with them. I also have nothing to report because we don't know what is wrong with her. My focus right now is Dallas and the babies. How is she feeling? Is she scared? The babies? Are they going to be fine? My kids are at home, I don't want them to worry, my two-year-old is asking for her mama and I don't know what to tell her. This is all a lot and until I get the info, I have nothing to tell anyone, except that she's in the hospital, and I don't know what's wrong.

When you have someone in the hospital and you have concerned friends and family, they all have a story, they all have to try to relate to you by telling you their story. I know they all mean well but it's exhausting.

"When I was sick, they did this."

"When I got my gallbladder taken out, they did this."

"When I broke my foot."

People love to give advice, they also love to be in the know especially when its bad news, they are right there wanting to know it all, with their sad faces and...

"Oh my gosh"

"I'm so sorry Hogi is there anything I can do to help"

The first few weeks everyone is rallying around you. People you haven't spoken to in years are calling and texting suddenly. Some people want to know because they are genuine, others because they are nosey, and then there are those who want to see something bad happen to me and my family. I know this seems a little harsh, but it happens, people like to see sadness, they like to watch the suffering. It's human nature. Doesn't make it right but it is the truth.

I am trying to maintain my composure, but no one understands. I don't need or want to hear the advice; I don't want to hear the stories. I need to know what is happening and I need to see my wife. I have very little patience and I am starting to get angry. It's best I don't respond to any messages right now

The rules at the hospital during COVID are, unless the patient is going to die then no one gets to visit, it's bullshit and I will be challenging it. I am a patient man but can only hold out for so long.

They will not allow me on the ward, I get any info from the nurses and from texts from Dallas.

Dec 3rd Dallas is in room T-427 at Community Regional medical center. I get a call from her nurse at 5am who gives me an update, she is sleeping and holding her own is the news today. They have decreased her oxygen so that is a good sign. The nurse told me.

"Hogi, she is one tough bitch "

I said.

"Yup that's my wife."

Then she said,

"Hogi, we have a diagnosis.

It's Pneumonia and its bad"

"Pneumonia",

I whisper under my breath.

My wife is 19 weeks pregnant with twins and has COVID and now pneumonia, viral pneumonia in all four quadrants of her lungs. I am trying to wrap my head around this. How can this be happening? It doesn't feel real. I am told the doctors are having a conference at 10 am. I still cannot be there, so I am waiting for them to call me when they are done.

I get the call at 5pm and the doctors tell me Dallas has eaten twice today and they are starting a second round of medications. I am told they are all safe for mom and babies. They are adding vitamins to her medications, Zinc, Vitamin C, Vitamin D. As long as they are safe for pregnant women, they are giving it to her. They have put her on a regular flow of oxygen to help with her breathing. I am starting to realize how bad this is. She is sick, very, very sick. I have to keep a level head, now more than ever she needs me.

Anything that can help get her immune system back up. I'm all for trying. She is mobile, she brushes her teeth, and uses the bathroom. All this is good to hear. I can talk to her, and she texts me throughout the day, so at least I have that. She is so tired, being sick and being pregnant it has drained her last ounce of energy. Now I must figure out how to see her. I carry on with my day and try not to get irritated, but the fact that I am unable to be with my wife and babies is extremely frustrating. I am starting to get angry now. Not sure who I need to contact but today I will be getting up on that ward. She is not going to do this alone. I try to sleep so I can be ready for the next day but it's impossible. I just lay there and think about my wife.

December 4th and another update, she is exhausted, they have increased her oxygen, so she is at 55%. She is resting but coughing up a lot of sputum and phlegm. I am told she is having a hard time catching her breath and I am starting to get worried. The nurses are very helpful, they are my lifeline right now, the only conduit between me and my wife is them. So, I am grateful when they update me.

The calls and texts from friends and family are still streaming in and I decide to give daily updates. I started documenting the daily events not just for my friends and family but for Dallas too. It is easier than trying to answer everyone individually. I just don't have time for that. I start in the morning after I speak with her nurse to see how her night went. I send the news to close family and friends; I then wait until the evening after I have been to the hospital and send out an end of day update. Of course, I'm still getting the questions, but it's few and far between on who I am responding to and it's exhausting. If I get any sort of negativity I don't answer, at this point that is the last thing I need, and it won't be tolerated.

I woke up to a call on December 5th. Dallas had a bad night and at 2:15 am she was ventilated, she requested this. The nurses gave her the choice, they said you make the call, if it's too much to try to keep breathing then make the call and we will do it, the nurse said it took her five minutes to make the decision. I wasn't privy to this conversation, but I understand because it means it got so bad there was no time to call me and discuss. I know she knows what's best so I am positive, but a ventilator? I'm not even sure I know what they do and how they work. Will she be out of it? Or still talking? Can she text me? Do they sedate her? Does it affect the babies? I didn't get to talk to her. We didn't get to discuss this. That's how I know, it was bad because she just did it.

Dr. Yang and nurse Jamie told me that she was working so hard to breathe that she could not take it anymore. They said she is comfortable now and slightly sedated and on pain meds to deal with the ventilator. She won't be texting me right now. A new rule has been implemented in the ICU that loved ones can visit a half hour a day. It's only a half hour but it's better than nothing at all. I can finally see my love and talk to the docs in person.

Progress
Chapter 3

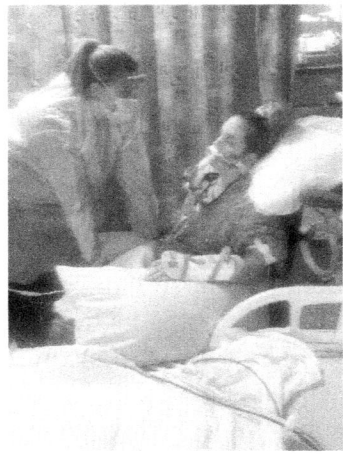

      I am able to see Dallas today. I have never seen anyone on a ventilator, so I don't really know what to expect. I'm nervous, but I have to stay strong for her.

      As I head to the ward, I am introduced to a doctor today. Her name is Dr. Crystal Ives Tolman, she is the head of the ECMO dept at Community Regional Medical Center. ECMO is Extracorporeal Membrane Oxygenation. She explains it to me but honestly, it's a lot to take in, it's a very complex procedure. Essentially this machine is a form of life support that takes over the heart and lung function of a patient, who is unable to provide an adequate amount of gas exchange or perfusion to sustain life,

I am not a doctor, I have never even had any type of surgery or procedure, so this is foreign to me, I understand what they are telling me, but it's a lot of information to process.

ECMO works by temporarily drawing blood from the body to allow artificial oxygenation of the red blood cells and removal of carbon dioxide. Dr. Ives tells me that Dallas is a good candidate for this. It is a very arduous procedure, extremely taxing on the body but is used in otherwise healthy individuals and she thinks it could really help Dallas.

I am not scared. I probably should be since ECMO is considered a type of life support. The term life support weighs heavy on my mind but again I am a man of facts and I take them, and I weigh them. I know that these doctors and nurses are the ones who know best, and if this will help Dallas get better and come home, then this is the route we will take. These people know what to do they have given their life to this and I have to trust the process.

I have no time for fear. I am now making all the decisions regarding my wife and unborn daughters. It is all on me and I cannot second guess. It is three lives that now hang in the balance. I have to think about everything and be level headed about everything I am told.

I take the information that Dr. Ives gives me and I listen intently. The mortality rate is 60% chance she could not make it on ECMO and the fact that she is pregnant with twins makes the mortality factor even higher. But the doctors don't know because they have never encountered this situation, which in fact should have frightened me to my core but it didn't, this was a unique situation, and I wasn't about to focus on the negative. To me ECMO was a Hail Mary, one last ditch effort to save her, but we weren't there yet, she was still holding her own on the ventilator and I had to be positive that she could turn this around. I have hope and I am holding on to that.

     I have spoken to the doctors and now I get to see her, I'm pumped, it's only been a few days but when you can't see your loved one it feels like months. Not long after Dallas went to the hospital Our nanny came down with strep, so I had no nanny, no one to keep Utley while I worked and went to the hospital to spend time with Dallas. I found out about a school from our friends, Bluff view preschool, they don't usually have any openings, very difficult to get into and you are put on a waitlist. I spoke with the director and told her what was going on and there was no hesitation, they registered Utley that day. I then called her best friend Christa; she lives in Bakersfield, and I knew she would drop everything to help me and Dallas. I needed someone who we both trusted. Dallas and I never leave our girl with strangers or sitters, it's either Christa, my mom or our nanny. Christa didn't hesitate, she dropped everything and moved into our barn and took over. She helped me get Utley ready in the morning and she would take her to school and pick her up if I could not. She would keep her occupied until I got back from the hospital and could get dinner ready and get Utley bathed and to bed.

At this point I don't know what to expect. I am prepping myself to see her. In general, I hate hospitals, I hate the smell, the machines, the germs, it makes me uncomfortable, but I can't focus on any of my own thoughts right now, I am here to see Dallas.

Before I can even see her, I have to go through the gowning up ritual. I dress in a full hazmat suit. The only visible part of my body is my eyes, and even then, there is a shield over them. I am saturated in sanitizer, my head and body are covered, I have gloves on my hands and coverings on my shoes, it takes a good twenty minutes before I can go to her room.

When I am brought in, I have to catch my breath for a second.

I whispered. "Holy shit" under my breath, I didn't expect to see her like this, she doesn't look like my Dallas. She is so very tired and sick; she was pale and she looked so sedated. I immediately went to her and took her hand and told her.

"Honey I'm here."

She squeezed my hand to signify that she heard me. I just looked at her and all I could think was this should have been me.

I'm told I can stay for a half-hour; this makes me laugh because they obviously do not know me and a half-hour isn't going to fly with me, but I will stay under the radar so I can hopefully get away with it. I am incredibly respectful of the nurses and doctors. If I earn their trust, they won't even notice I am here.

As I said, a half hour turned into 1.5 hours, she is coherent, and I can correspond with her via white board she is all business of course. Making sure I was taking care of everything. Her spirits were good and that is what counts. I need her to stay positive. It almost like she knew I would be nervous, and she calmed me instead of the other way around. I kissed her when I leave and tell her I love her, and I will be back tomorrow. She tries to smile and squeezes my hand.

The doctor calls me later the same evening. They have decided to reduce her sedation because she is starting to outwork her ventilator. Her blood pressure is good and vitals are all stable, they fed her dinner and gave her meds, and reported that my babies were very active.

I am happy to hear all this, but emotionally and physically I am exhausted. I'm still not sleeping; I try but it's not happening. I stay up doing laundry, cleaning the house, feeding the animals, pacing the grounds at all hours of the day and night. Anything to keep my mind occupied. If you had told me a month ago this would be my life, I would have told you, you were batshit crazy, but here we are.

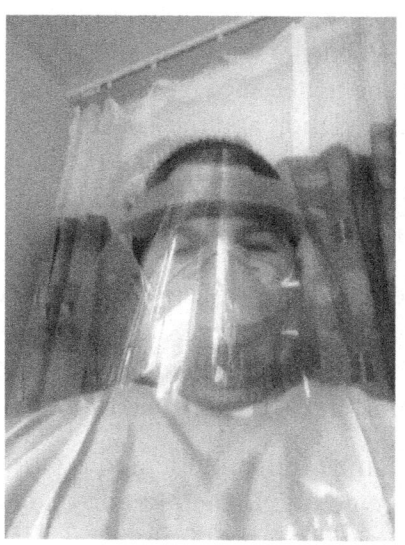

Waiting
Chapter 4

This morning I woke to a text from my wife. This is a great sign. I called the nurse for a report on the night and she said they were very happy with her progress through the night, and they have reduced her oxygen again down to 50%. She slept until 4am. When she woke up, she asked for her phone and she texted me right away. They have lowered her sedation and they have given her some pain meds to get her through having the ventilator. It is a tube going down your throat into your lungs so it must be uncomfortable and painful.

She sent me a grocery list, so I knew then that she was feeling better. She is making sure I am staying on point. So, I can smile about that. I can't help but think she is turning a corner?

December 6th and I am going to visit again. My visits are getting longer, but no one is saying anything to me. I don't care if they do, I'm not going anywhere. And they are starting to realize this. I spoke with her doctors in person today and they are happy with her progress. We are not out of the woods yet, and they make me aware of this, but so far everything is going in the right direction. They did an ultrasound, so I got to see my girls, they are healthy and moving around so I hold onto that and thank God.

Each day is like Groundhog Day. I try to sleep, I am so restless and tired, but I can't stop my mind from spinning. So, I try to keep myself occupied, I have to be strong, not just for her, but for my kids at home, my family, and for myself. I can't dwell on the what ifs so I'm keeping my circle small. If anyone texts me or calls and starts in on the negative, I cut them off. I have no time nor the patience for it. In times like these you truly get to see who your true friends are, I have people I haven't spoken to in years calling and texting me still and I know they don't really care they just want to know what's happening. I have realized in my life that people thrive on drama, they are not hoping for the best, they are thinking the worst and they are nosey. This is a small town everyone talks. They have no clue what I'm going through, and I can't even explain it. I don't have anyone to talk to that can understand. I can't talk to Dallas, she is my everything, my best friend, my person. It's like a nightmare and I can't seem to wake up.

It's December 7th, I have come to the conclusion that the ICU is not a place I want to be. Everyone is treating me with kid gloves, they truly do not know me yet, I can tell. I am not the guy that sits quietly in the corner and reads scripture to his wife. I am the guy that gets everything moving. I am the guy that tells them what is going on. Keeps everyone on their toes, I am not the sit and wait guy, I want answers and I want results and I want them yesterday.

I walk into the ICU today and I see her eyes and I know immediately she is panicking. I look at the monitor and her heart rate is doubling. Now I am pissed, the gloves are coming off today. I am now introducing them to who I really am and trust me they don't want to meet this guy. The doctor was talking to me and trying to calm me down and all I heard was him sounding like a teacher from Charlie Brown, I told him very directly.

"I do not give a fuck what your thoughts are "you need to give her something to relax."

He heard me loud and clear, and they gave her some more sedation and got her heart rate down. They think I don't know my wife and they need to know that I know her better than anyone; I can feel it when I walk in the room, I can tell by the look in her eye, I can sense it and I'll be damned if I let some doctor who just met her tell me what he thinks is happening. I know what is happening and we are fixing this. Today they met me, the real Hogi, I am no longer flying under the radar keeping a low profile. They have now met the guy who does not give a shit what people think, I say what I say and if you do not like it then walk away. I will not back down; this is my life, my wife, my daughters. I control this.

She has taken two steps backward. I was prepared for this. She is working overtime and she is pregnant, the babies are getting everything, they are thriving, so she must fight twice as hard just to catch a break. They have upped her oxygen to 60. I stayed all day and helped with her PT, and just held her hand so she would know I was there. They need to keep her moving so PT is crucial. By the time I was leaving she was back down to 50%. She overdid it, so I took her phone and told her she had to rest. The docs are trying to wean her off sedation, but she has some delirium. Apparently, this is normal for someone who is ventilated and sedated. She is not making sense and getting her days and nights mixed up. I had to inform my family and friends that if she texts or calls them, they are to tell her to go back to sleep. Do not engage and keep it short, she is confused.

December 8th, and I pushed my luck today. I stayed for over 6 hours. No one asked me to leave so I stayed until someone noticed and told me it was time. Dr. Vangandy came in to check her and she said she is getting better, albeit slowly. Her oxygen levels have stayed at 50% these last few days and her saturation is at 94%. This is stable according to them. I held her today while she slept, it is all I could do. I needed her to know I was there and I would protect her. I just had her in my arms and whispered how much I love her in her ear and that I want her to come home. When I was leaving, she wrote me a note that said,

"When can I go home?"

It broke my heart to read this, but I told her very matter of fact when she stops thinking and gets off her phone and gets some sleep she will mend faster and then I can take her home.

December 9th, I woke up this morning to find my wife had posted on Instagram. She won't remember it. This is not her. She is so private, and I know it doesn't make much sense. The pictures she put were crazy, and her captions were not anything she would write. I get to the hospital, and I take her phone and delete the posts. I call her friends and family who see it and let them know that she is out of it and that please do not start messaging her, she will get overwhelmed quickly and she doesn't need that. The posts were not her; she is not in her right mind.

You don't realize when a patient is on a ventilator and they are highly medicated, it affects their psychosis in such a strange way. She thinks she knows what's happening, but she is so confused. She doesn't know day from night right now and her thoughts are all over the place. She gets very upset over minor things. I cannot do anything but be patient with her. I can't get upset because I know it's not her right now, I just keep her calm and get her to rest. It's another story to tell her when she comes home.

The days are starting to run into one another every day is the same. I don't know if it's Tuesday or Saturday. If I sleep it's for short periods, never straight through. My house has never been cleaner. I am concerned about my daughter, but she seems fine. We talk about mom all the time, I show her pictures. We play and laugh together. She wakes in the morning and goes looking for her mom. How do you tell a two-year-old that her mommy is very sick? I just told her; mommy is down the street at a resort getting some rest. That little girl keeps me sane. My sons are doing ok. Evan is taking it the hardest. He loves Dallas and he is always worried about me. He thinks I spread myself too thin. For a 16-year-old he has so much wisdom. And he cares so much about me. Hogi 5 is like me, stoic, does not like to show feelings, but he is there every night for dinner, and he checks in on me daily. He helps me when I need him to watch Utley or run to the store for me. I must be strong for them, I want them to see strength and positivity, not sadness and negativity. It's the hardest thing I have had to do to pretend this isn't affecting me as badly as it is. I am grateful that Utley is only 2years old, it means she will never remember the winter of 2020.

December 10th, I am headed back to the hospital, Christa is here with Utley, so I can head up for the day. I never really know what I am walking into, but I am just happy to get to see her. If I am having a bad day, I just know that once I see Dallas, I feel better. She lights me up. Even when she doesn't even know I am there, I just immediately feel better to be by her side.

The nurses have had her doing physical therapy. She has been crushing it. Being bedridden is not good for lung injured patients. All the fluids tend to sit and fester, so they need her moving to keep her blood flowing. She is a strong woman so I expect nothing less. The doctors are happy with her progress, and they let me know this, so I feel like we could be at a turning point. Her vent is at 40%

with 8 % pressure. The babies continue to thrive, and I get to see them daily, so it eases my stress a little. I know my wife is doing everything she can for these babies.

I have to say the doctors and nurses here are so incredible. It is evident how serious they take their jobs, and I am so grateful for this. I decided I had to do something to show them my gratitude.

I start ordering them food. These people work effortlessly every day, putting themselves in harm's way to spend 12 hours with my wife away from their own families. So, every day I call a local food joint and I order lunch and dinner for the entire ward staff. This is such a small act, but I have to do something. I need to show my gratitude to them. My wife's nurse Ashley cries when she updates me about her, it really affects her and to see the concern and care in her eyes makes me realize that she is in a good place and that she is in good hands. This is a totally new experience, not just for me but for everyone here, A woman pregnant with twins with COVID and no one knows the outcome. No one has experienced this situation before, but they are being so positive with me and so hands on with Dallas, I could not ask for more.

I have a lot of people questioning if she is in good hands. There is always the question if she should be transferred to Stanford or UC Davis where they have more experience and better doctors, my answer is a resounding no. She is in the best care with the best doctors and nurses, and this is where she is staying.

Turning A Corner
Chapter 5

    The doctors are looking to start weaning Dallas off the ventilator. She is down to 40% and they are looking to get her down to 35% today. Today was a rough day for her. She was not in good spirits and it takes all of me to change that. I need to be her rock and keep her going. This is difficult because she is a very strong-willed woman, so I need to help her keep up the fight. I have no idea what she is going through. She can't talk, and she is still confused so I try so hard not to let her give up. It's not going to happen and If I have to be the bad guy and push her like hell, then so be it. I have to put my feelings on the backburner when I am with her, because anything I am going through doesn't compare to her life right now.

    December 11th the doctors are having her relax today. They think she has overdone it, so a day off is needed. Everything is the same. Vitals and oxygen remain stable, but sleep is what she needs right now. Her coughing has subsided so, again I am looking at all of this and I am happy. The doctors have told me this is not a sprint but a marathon, hard for a guy like me to hear. I like results getting things done swiftly and effectively is how I live my life. This situation has taught me I have zero control and it's harder than I thought, there is no magic wand to wave to make her come back, no one to give her a potion to make her better, it's a lesson in patience and strength and resilience and so far, I have risen to the challenge.

This morning I got a call from my cousin and business partner Mark, his dad and my uncle Walt had passed away. I am heartbroken. Walt was a wonderful man and I loved him deeply, and I know he loved me. He got sick around the same time as Dallas. He too tested positive for COVID-19, just like Dallas his COVID turned into pneumonia and before we knew it, he was also on a ventilator. He was actually on the same ward as Dallas, but I was not able to visit with him. He was not a candidate for ECMO, it is such an intense treatment that you can die from the treatment itself. It is used in younger adults who have a chance of making it through. He didn't fit the criteria for it and it kills me that he couldn't be saved.

I need to be there for Mark and his family, on top of being there for my own. I have to help him with the funeral and just be there for him emotionally and physically to help out with work, he is going to need time off. Mark and his dad were best friends and it's going to take some time for him to heal from this. Another bump in the road I am travelling right now, and I feel a little beaten down.

Tonight was a quiet night. The doctors decided to push her sedation up because she was fighting to rest. She wants to be awake and alert so badly, but she cannot heal this way. I was asked about the impossible today. They asked me to stay away. I understand this is for her benefit, but it does not make it any easier for me. I comply but only because I know it's what she needs. Today I will keep busy with my kids so I can keep my mind occupied and not stress about the fact that I am not by her side. It will allow me to be with Mark and his family and get caught up on some work.

The next few days are a blur. She is staying stable but still not getting better. When she is lucid, she gets angry and upset so they have to sedate her some more. It's a vicious cycle. Because I want her to come out of this, I want her to fight like hell and come back to me, but I also know that this is a waiting game. Her body is being ravaged with infection right now. The doctors readily admit this is new to them. COVID is so new and the fact that she now has pneumonia and is carrying two children, this is a whole new ball game. I have no one to say,

"Oh Yes Mr. Selling, we had a patient just like this last year and she made a full recovery "everything will be alright."

They truly do not know what the outcome of this will be. It has never happened. If I think about it, it will consume me. The only outcome I am looking for is taking my wife and babies' home.

Everything Changed
Chapter 6

December 12th, there is no way around it. It's terrible, another X-RAY and her pneumonia has not gotten better. No improvement. I am beside myself, what are we doing? How is this possible? It's been 12 days and she has been ventilated for 10 of them. This was supposed to help her, let the ventilator breathe for her to rest her lungs, not make it worse. Her ventilator is now up at 65%, the highest it's been so far. They have sedated her even more to keep her rested. We are losing this battle.

ECMO was mentioned again if things don't change quickly, it will have to be done. I am so angry inside; my blood is boiling. I must fight again with the hospital heads to get up there. They are saying I need to stay away. I made it clear on the phone that I will be there tomorrow, and I will not accept anything but an open door. I am praying, I am praying harder than I ever have before.

December 13th Utley slept with me last night. I needed that. She is my savior right now. She is so sweet and innocent, and I cannot let her know what is going on, she can't see me lose it, I am all she has right now. None of my kids can see me lose it. Surprisingly I slept too, maybe it was having my little one next to me, knowing she is safe and next to me, and I can protect her from this roller coaster. I try so hard not to let her see me upset, she is too young to know what is truly happening, but I know she misses her mom and does not understand where she is. All she has is me right now, and I will protect her with every fiber of my being.

December 13th Proning, this is when they flip a lung patient onto their stomach. Physical position affects the distribution and volume of air in the patient's lungs. This can have a direct effect on the expansion or collapse of the alveoli that permit the exchange of oxygen and carbon dioxide in the blood. Apparently, lying Supine (on the back) can be detrimental to pulmonary function, especially in patients who are on mechanical ventilation. In supine position patients' lungs are compressed by gravity and other forces, including internal organs. The supine position can cause hyperinflation of the alveoli in the ventricular (upward facing) lung while causing alveolar collapse in the dorsal part of the lung. I did a lot of research in order to write all that.

Obviously when I was told they wanted to prone her, I needed to research as much as possible. I had no idea what it was or why they would consider it. Putting a pregnant woman on her stomach didn't seem like a great idea to me, having all that weight pushing on her belly seemed more dangerous than helpful. But I'm not the doctor so I trust they know what they are doing.

The doctors told me that putting Dallas on her stomach will increase her ventilation of the dorsal lung region which is the base of her lungs where the fluid is sitting. The benefits are a more even distribution of ventilator volumes and pressure throughout the lung, which can also reduce the severity of lung injury due to being ventilated. Will it help is all I care about; I will try anything at this point.

    I headed to Target to buy pillows, yes pillows. I was told since she is pregnant the more pillows to ease the transition of putting pressure on her abdomen will help. So, I bought a ton of pillows and brought them to the hospital.

    I was allowed back in, so I went to see her. She was highly sedated, so I just sat there and held her hand. I took a bible and a cross I was given by a dear friend Jen Lloren. I placed the Bible on her chest and the cross on her head. I told her about what's been going on, talked to her about Utley and the boys. I know in my heart she can hear me and that it will calm her. I told her I love her, and I miss her and that I would do anything for her and to please keep fighting for herself and the girls.

    I did this for two hours and then they asked me to leave. It's time to prone her. They will move her to her stomach for 16 hours a day then back on her back for 8, they will do this every day to allow for better ventilation. The babies are great, and they assure me proning will not adversely affect them. The nurses felt them kicking and rolling around inside mom. It makes my heart happy to hear them talk about how active they are.

Dr. Ives wants to speak to me, this woman is the epitome of a stud. She is so knowledgeable and has a wealth of information. She mentions ECMO again, she explains the process to me again and tells me we won't go this direction unless the ventilator needs to be upped and the proning doesn't work. In a nutshell they want the proning to work, but they want me to know my options. Because they make no guarantees. I feel like she is telling me this because she knows this is the direction it is going, and she needs me to get prepared.

My friends and family are rallying around me right now. One of my dear friends started a meal train for my family. It's so incredibly thoughtful, but it's not me. I accept it for about a week, then ask for it to cease. I just want my kids around me and everything at home to be as normal as possible. I don't want to see a lot of people right now; I don't have the energy. I lean on my mom a lot and a very close cousin in Texas. They listen to me, they don't give advice except the standard, make sure you're eating and try to sleep. They don't know what to do or say and honestly nothing they do or say can make any of this better, but I appreciate them for being there for me and listening. My mom texts and calls me every day just to check on me and I greatly appreciate her for that.

I know I have been short with people, and I apologize for it when it happens. I am emotionally drained, and my patience is running thin and on top of that I am very angry.

Anyone that knows me, knows I do not take my problems out on others. I am not a talker. I hunker down, and I deal with the hand I'm dealt. But honestly, I don't even know how to deal with this. At this point every day is a gamble. One day things look good and the next I'm questioning whether I have to prepare myself for the worst.

ECMO
Chapter 7

December 13th, Proning didn't work, they managed five hours and realized quickly it was hurting her more than helping. She is too far gone; she is just too sick and it's not going to help her.

They are trying a left and right lateral recumbent now, just to keep her mobile. That is moving her from side to side rather than flipping her over. Her ventilator is at 80%, it has risen in the last week, which is indicative that the pneumonia is ravaging her. Now I am scared. I feel like we keep going backward. She has a fever again and she is sedated even more. I haven't talked to her in what seems like forever.

The babies continue to thrive, which is impressive to me. Looking at Dallas laying there hooked up to so many machines, a feeding tube, so sick, it is a wonder that the babies have not been affected by any of it. My girls are beyond strong, and it amazes me.

December 14th Today's update was that she has rested through the night, she is highly sedated to keep her resting and calm. One of my friends called and asked for an update, to see if I was good, we chatted for a bit and he said if I needed a break and wanted to go for a drink to give him a call. It dawned on me then that I had not had a drink or chew in 11 weeks. It is not a huge deal; I haven't ever had a problem with drinking or chewing. I enjoyed it, a good stress reliever, but I never took it to excess, but randomly 11 weeks ago, I just stopped. I don't know why. I just didn't want it anymore. Maybe in some way it was foreshadowing of what was to be in my life. Something was telling me I needed to have a clear mind and be the healthiest version of myself that I could be. If you had told me, it was because my wife and children were in peril, and they could die. I would have never believed you.

This morning I was supposed to go to the hospital at my usual time, around 9:30, but today something in my gut told me to go early, I felt something was wrong. So, at 6 am I made my way to the hospital. As I walked into Dallas's room Dr Ives and Dr Evans the heads of the ECMO team were there. I knew this was it, today was the day. They told me Dallas vitals were good, but the problem is the CO_2 in her lungs was rising way too fast. She has been on Lasix which is a diuretic to get rid of all the excess fluid in her body and it was not working. She started running a temperature again and the doctors were running labs to check her white blood cells to see if there was something else going on. As a precaution they started her on antibiotics until the lab results came back.

The decision was made then and there, we would start ECMO today. That is when I truly knew it was bad, really bad, 10 days on a ventilator and she is getting worse. From the research I have done on ECMO since it was first mentioned to me, it is a last-ditch attempt, when all else has failed they pull out the ECMO and throw a Hail Mary. When Dr Ives said it was time, I said.

"What are we waiting for?"

VV ECMO, Veno Venous ECMO is primarily used for lung function vs VA ECMO which is for heart and lung. Dallas is getting the VV ECMO, for her lungs. I am told they will start the procedure after lunch, they need to book an OR and once done they will send her back to ICU. I am not allowed to see her until tomorrow. I am at a loss for words, this is what it has come to. I have updated my friends and family and just asked that they pray for my wife and babies. Just pray. I Have nothing else to say

I am waiting again; the procedure was supposed to be performed at 12:30 pm and it is now 4:1 pm and they are just now taking her back to the OR. The waiting is killing me, and the fact that I can't wait at the hospital makes it ten times worse. 5:45pm and Dr. Ives calls me, she did great, she received the Cannulae, it was placed in her neck and they are moving her back to her room to start the process.

Is It Working?
Chapter 8

It is 5 am on December 15th and I just got off the phone with Dallas nurse. Last night her ventilator was at 90% and the ECMO was at 4.0 which is the highest setting. This morning she is at 1.5 on ECMO and the ventilator is down to 50%. I am ecstatic to hear this. It's been less than 12 hours and improvement is happening. I truly had no idea what to expect, like I have said so many times, the doctors also have no idea. This truly was a shot in the dark and so far, it's working. I am keeping only positive thoughts in my mind.

Her nurse said they bathed her and brushed her hair and that the babies were moving around like crazy. I love hearing this. The nurses have so much pride in my babies. They are always updating me about their movement, always putting their hands on Dallas's belly to make sure the girls are active. They are very invested, and it truly warms my heart to see and hear.

We are back to half hour visits again, but I don't care. At least I am allowed. I stayed longer of course, but I'm not pushing it. I want to come back, so I abide by their rules.

Today she looked puffy, the nurse said it was due to the blood transfusion she received yesterday while they were inserting the Cannulae. I see that it is in her neck and she now has more tubes and machinery. I should be used to it by now, but I am not. It's hard to see, it's hard to watch the woman I love like this. She doesn't even look like the same person. This illness has hit her so hard.

They tried to lower her sedation, but Dallas decided she wanted to sit up. So, they had to up it again so she would not do that. When she gets erratic and won't stay calm, they have to restrain her, so I am hoping I can talk to her and keep her calm.

December 16th more waiting, nothing has changed today, they are trying to lower her pain meds because she seems to be tolerating everything quite well. The nurses said the ECMO team has been raising the sweep up and down accordingly to remove the CO_2. They told me this is very important within the first 12-36 hours. It will show how much her body can withstand and they adjust it accordingly.

The Babies
Chapter 9

Today I had to speak with the Obstetrics team about the girls. It was a horrifying conversation to have to have, but one I know needed to be discussed. I was asked today if the babies are in trouble and I need to choose between saving them or saving my wife. What was my choice? This is a question no man wants to answer. This is my wife, the mother of my little girl at home, and these are my babies who I have never met but love more than humanly possible.

100% save my wife was my answer, without her there are no babies. I did not waiver from answering this. It is not just that, I cannot fathom our daughter at home growing up without a mother. It has plagued my thoughts in the last three weeks, and I cannot deal with it. I inform my friends and family about this decision. I know I don't have too, it's none of anyone's business, but I know the question is wanting to be asked. This may not be what people want to hear, but I don't care, it's my decision and I made it. Done, no questions asked.

I cried today, probably the first time since this has all happened, it's overwhelming, I am making decisions for three. It's a lot on my shoulders, and it also dawned on me that I could lose all three. I am being asked to choose, when in reality I may not have a choice at all. I can't stop thinking about Utley not having a mom. It kills me, and I just can't handle the thought. I can't lose them.

We chose names for the girls before all this happened. Harvee and Hayze, unconventional names I know, but we are unconventional people, my name is Holger, it doesn't get more different than that. It makes me happy that we named them before all of this took place. I don't just refer to them as Baby A and Baby B. They are my daughters, and they have names. I went so far as to have their names tattooed on my hands. No matter what happens I have two daughters, their names are Harvee and Hayze Selling.

The Long Road Ahead
Chapter 10

December 17th, I met a new doctor today, Dr Pool. She went through the ECMO procedure with me again. Told me about the process of the continued sweeping of the lungs and how my wife's body is reacting to it. Dr Pool was very direct, in telling me that this is a long process due to her lungs being previously damaged. This sickness only exposed the underlying damage and brought it to the forefront. She told me to be patient, I was getting sick of being told that, but I kept quiet and listened. She explains again like the others that this is a marathon not a sprint.

Dr. Pool explains that not hearing from the team is a good sign and to not worry about it. I did not receive that information well, and I retorted, the team needs to make a concentrated effort to keep me informed, good or bad. I am allowed to visit once a day and I am abiding to that, but not getting updates was unacceptable. She understood and agreed to keep me informed no matter what the news may be.

December 17th I am shown a new X-RAY of Dallas' lungs, there is a slight difference in the lower quadrant of her lungs from the last X-RAY that was done on the 14th. A slight improvement was better than no improvement. They also performed an ultrasound on the girls while I was there, seeing the twins always makes the day better for me, those girls are kicking up a storm and their heartbeats are nice and high.

They have decided to reduce Dallas' sedation slowly. Dallas gets very excited and tries to move around which is good and bad, the nurses work with her vocally to try to keep her calm. Whenever I am there, it gets worse, I know it's because she is trying to communicate with me. She desperately wants to talk to me, but she can't. So, I do my best to keep her calm. I talk to her quietly in her ear, so she knows I am close and I hold her hand to make her relax, and for her to know that it's all going to be ok. It usually works, and then the staff usually ask me to leave shortly after so it doesn't happen again, and she can get some sleep. I comply and head home to my kids for the night.

December 18^{th,} I called the hospital at 4:30 am and was told Dallas did not have a good night. She was extremely restless; she was trying to pull out her tubes. They explained to me that this is normal. I know this should not make me happy, but it does, it means she knows what's up and she is trying to speed things up in her own Dallas fashion. My wife is a hard ass and I know she won't take any of this in stride, she wants to come home and is fighting to get there. I am however a little tired of everyone telling me it's normal. This is so far from any normal that I have experienced.

Another conversation with the OB doctor's Dr. Pelletier and Dr Morgan, in a nutshell besides daily ultrasounds, they want to start monitoring the babies on the 27th of December. This means that Dallas would be wearing a daily monitor. This would mean that if they saw any issues whatsoever, I would have to decide to take the babies. She is only 22 weeks pregnant. The babies could be born now, it would be a lot though. If it was one, it's a different story. But we have two and as of now they only weigh approximately one pound each. My heart and mind tell me it's too soon. But I need to be prepared. I didn't take the conversation well, they told me once again that this will be a long process and that I need to slow down. This is dwelling on the negative and the what if's and I don't want to hear it. I had to walk away and catch my breath and collect my thoughts and come back to the conversation.

I can say without trepidation that this has been the worst experience of my life, with the best people. These people genuinely care. They are wearing this, and I cannot even begin to know how hard it is to deal with these situations daily. And I am grateful. I know I am not the easiest person to deal with, but they understand that and are still willing to help me and listen to my daily rants.

More Waiting
Chapter 11

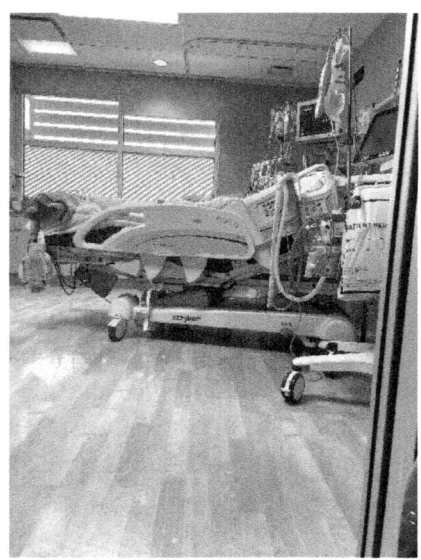

   I am still going through the motions; we are five days away from Christmas, and it does not seem like we are any closer to Dallas coming out of this. Every day is the same report, she is stable. The ECMO is still working, and she is still on the Ventilator. All that and there is still no change, she is still highly sedated. The doctors have been actively trying to find a combination of drugs that will allow her to come out of sedation, but thus far nothing has worked. She gets highly agitated, especially when I am there. I do the usual, sit with her and hold her hand and talk to her. I tell her about Utley and how she loves school and the songs she sings and how she is obsessed with band aids right now. I tell her about work, how I go everyday to the job sites and all the new jobs coming in, I just talk, but she still gets very irritated, and they end up having to sedate her all over again to calm her back down.

The news today is her CO_2 levels are dropping, and her vitals are all stable. This means the ECMO is doing its job. The PT department wants to meet with me to discuss the future. There are a lot of options, and we need to make sure we have all the decisions made so she can get to it when she gets through this. As of now it's futile. She is still so sick, so I feel like we are spinning our wheels, discussing the future. It is focusing on the positive which I am grateful for, and I know we have to do it, but right now I just want all the tubes out and to have her breathing again on her own.

Dr. Ives tells me today that I look tired. She is correct, I am. I am exhausted. This is not just an emotional battle, it is a physical one. The less sleep I get, the more irritable I am. I am beat down. I still have a business to run, kids to raise, and a house to take care of, along with all this madness. I do not have anyone to help me. Yes, I have friends who are there for me. They check in daily, and they ask if I need anything, or if I am ok. But how do you say No I am not? I am not ok; I don't know if I will be ok again. I do not know what my life is going to look like tomorrow. I am living minute by minute right now. I am trying to keep my head high, but I am being beat down at every turn. How do you tell your friends or family that you're scared?

You don't! You can't, because there is no room for fear right now. I cannot be scared. I can't worry. I can't lose my shit. Everyone is depending on me to keep it together. I can't fold now, so I do what the doctor says. I go home to my kids and we all have ice cream. We smile and laugh for a moment, and for a brief moment, I can smile and laugh, and be grateful for these children in my life that are keeping me strong.

Business
Chapter 12

While all this madness is ongoing in my personal life, I tend to forget I still have a business to run. A few of them, my primary being an electrical company. This has been my primary business for the last twenty-five years. I also own a bar, and a restaurant. I have partners in all these endeavors. But I have always been hands-on, the forefront of the company. I am a hands-on leader. I go to all my jobs. I talk to my employees all the time and I am the first to get to work in the morning. I will sometimes head to the office at 3 am just to get my day started, this was no different just because Dallas was in the hospital, my days just got longer is all.

Now, I no longer just have my own business to worry about, I have hers. As a family law attorney, she deals with divorces, child custody, paternity, property division, domestic violence and restraining orders. I realized that I had to contact her staff, and we needed to talk. I planned a meeting with them all so I could fill them in on what was happening and figure out what to do. When she first went in, she was still able to access emails and talk to her team via email. Now she can't even talk to me, never mind reading emails and responding to clients. The doctors are telling me that this could take six months to a year for her to recover and we do not know what kind of residual effect she will have. I had no idea how many clients she had or cases she was in the middle of, and they needed to know now that she would not be handling anything.

    I met with the office assistant and paralegal. I found out there were approximately 140 clients being represented by her law firm. I didn't know what to do, so I contacted the bar to get some guidance. I was told we needed to send out substitution letters and refund all clients from the IOLTA account. I didn't even know what that was. I had to go through all her accounts and close out the month of November. I had to pay all the bills and do payroll. I stayed in contact with all her employees, and I made deposits, but inevitably we would have to close down. The bar states that only a licensed attorney can hold a law firm, even though she was still licensed, I knew she wasn't going back. We had no idea what the repercussions of her illness would be and the fact that she was giving birth to twins, and we have a two-year-old at home, it was too much of a gamble. I can't talk to Dallas about this, she is not coherent, she is in no place to make any type of decision. It's all on me, I have to make this decision and when and if she comes out of this, I have to explain to her that she no longer has a law firm. I have decided to leave the office clean out to her, she will need that when she gets out, to have some control over the situation. It was a difficult decision, but I had to do it. We were working minute by minute and my last concern in life was whether she would have a job at the end of all this. At this point I just wanted her to live.

Currently, Dallas is the one who handles all our finances. She takes care of home and kids and I work and take care of the yard and animals; I realize I do not have any passwords to get into any of our accounts, I don't have any way of paying our bills, something as simple as our electricity bill and I don't have access. I completely forgot, and I was seeing the mail pile up and realized they were bills, I can't even get cash out of our bank account because I don't have passwords to those either. Christa and I decide she must pretend to be Dallas and say she has forgotten our passcodes for me to pay all our bills. It works and I now have to go through everything and make sure everything is paid and up to date.

Turning A Corner
Chapter 13

It's the 19th of December, The ECMO settings are down to 2.9 and they are changing out her pain meds; she was on propofol, which is hardcore. She was basically in a medically induced coma to deal with it all; they want her to be more alert, to start coming back, so they are changing to Skelaxin which is more of a muscle relaxer rather than a type of anesthesia. I have been reassured that these drugs will not affect the babies.

With her ECMO settings going down and the docs wanting her to be more alert, I am feeling like we are going to see some changes.

The doctors here continue to amaze me daily, they are brilliant, and half the time, I don't understand what they are saying, but I know they are doing what is best, and giving the best treatment. It must be intimidating for them; they have never had someone pregnant with twins so sick and on a ventilator and on ECMO. They have never dealt with COVID before, so this is all new to them and to me. They honestly can't assure me that the outcome of this will go in my favor, but they are upbeat, and they are in it for the long haul, right next to me.

Along with the names of my twin girls on my hands, I had HOLD FAST tattooed on my fingers. I know it sounds crazy, my wife is in the hospital, and I'm going to get tattoos, but it held so much meaning, I read it and I knew immediately it was meant to be. HOLD FAST means to bear down and fight through the storm, you will not only survive the storm, you will be stronger because of how you made it through. Continue to believe in or adhere to an idea or principle, it means you stand with your convictions, your truth, your gut and your heart. HOLD FAST to your inner voice and be proud to have the strength to be your own person. This resonated with me so strongly with what I have been going through, it spoke to me. Some people go to therapy, I get tattoos.

      I spent 3.5 hours at the hospital today. I have started bringing donuts to all the wards, again a small token of my appreciation for all these people who are on the front line. I see they appreciate it and that is all that matters. Her ECMO settings have been reduced again and her ventilator is at 25%. They have started to give her Seroquel, it's an antipsychotic, due to her being sedated for so long she is having trouble coming out of it. This should ease the transition, I hope. I was happy that she was sleeping while I visited today, with no fireworks and lots of rest. Another X-RAY was done, and her lungs are healing, it's a slow process, but it's good to see there is some. The doctors are great about showing me everything, her X-RAYS and test results, they show me each X-RAY to see the differences. They are good about keeping involved.

December 20th, we are five days from Christmas, and I am trying to be excited for my kids. I wish we could have a sense of normalcy, but there is nothing normal about this Christmas. Utley isn't aware of the extreme nature of her mom's illness. I am grateful for that, she doesn't need to know about this, it's too much for even me to deal with, never mind a child. I have taken her to Candy Cane Lane a few times, so she feels the Christmas spirit, even though her dad wants to get it done and over with. It helps to take her places; she has such a pure heart and such innocence, she loves the simple things that as we get older, we take for granted. Just looking at Christmas lights amazes her, and it makes me smile. For a minute I can forget what is happening all around me and be happy and content with my little girl.

I wasn't allowed in the room today to see Dallas. Coming out of sedation is proving harder than we anticipated, so they ask me to step out. Some days, they do not want me in at all because she is in such an agitated state when I am there. When days like this happen, I sit outside until they ask me to leave. They don't even argue with me anymore because they know I am not going anywhere. I'll sit outside her room all day if I have to.

December 21st, I just talked to Dallas nurse Cathy; she told me they had found a good cocktail of drugs for her to come out of sedation. I am happy to hear this but will believe it when I see it. They brushed her teeth and braided her hair. I am grateful she is not coherent right now because she hates braids, she would be so pissed. So, I took a picture so she can hopefully laugh at this later. I am holding on to the little things, so when she wakes up, I can show her what she went through, all of it, the good, the bad, the ugly. I just pray I get the chance.

I just got home from the hospital, and it was a good day; they had her sit up today and do some PT, she didn't lose her cool today, so I think their cocktail of drugs is working. The head of ECMO doctor came by and they are looking to take her off ECMO tonight. They showed me her X-RAYS and they have improved a lot in the last 3 days. You can see where there are now clear areas, whereas before it just looked ravaged with fluid and infection. I am no doctor, but you could see an improvement. I am glad they show me these things, it helps a lot to get to see it, rather than have someone tell you about it. I need to see it. I will get the call today between 3 and 4 o'clock pm for their decision.

Today was a great day and it's the 21st. All I know is that 21 is my favorite number, so knowing that today could be the day she is removed from ECMO is huge.

Almost There
Chapter 14

December 22nd, it is 6:20 am, and I have been waiting at the hospital for over an hour. The doctors let me know last night they are taking her off ECMO, the room is prepped, and we are just waiting. I have been sitting in the hospital cafeteria for what seems like days. It is unbelievable to me; this whole month has been a blur, there are times when I have just gone through the motions and when things slow down, I really think, oh my God, this is insane. My wife has been on her deathbed, we had no idea the outcome of this, so taking out the ECMO is such a huge step. It means she is getting better. This is all I have prayed for.

After researching ECMO, this could have been so bad, don't get me wrong, it was a bad, horrific event, ECMO is so touch and go. Some people do well on it, others end up dying and getting pregnant on top of it. It is a blessing really that the babies made it, a miracle that Dallas made it this far.

10:57 am ECMO has been removed. This is huge, she still has the ventilator, but it's only at 50% and they say they can lower it again this afternoon. Now that ECMO is gone, her lungs have healed a great deal and the probability of getting rid of the ventilator is high. She has been on the ventilator for 20 days now, it's unreal, 20 days of something helping you live, 20 days of being fed through a tube, not seeing your family, and maybe not remembering a thing.

The ECMO is gone, the "Hail Mary" was successful. I know we aren't out of the woods yet, but she is still alive, and my babies are still alive. So, to me, this is a huge win. Her vitals are all good and her color is the best I have seen in 20 days, she actually has some color in her cheeks.

I got to see the baby's heartbeats and they are strong at 158 and 164. I took some pics this morning, again just for Dallas. I was told she wouldn't remember any of this, once she went dark, her memory gets wiped. If she wants to share with people at a later date, then that will be her choice. I am a private guy, and I would never post anything or show anyone anything without her consent. But I think it is a good idea to show her when this is all said and done. It's insane to me that she will have no memory of this; I am glad she won't, but it's also so wild to think that she can be completely unaware of any of this going on.

The meeting with the OB docs was informative, to say the least, they want to put more monitoring on the girls. This may sound completely bizarre to a lot of people, but I said no, if Dallas is not healthy enough to have a C- section safely, then I don't want it. If they monitor the babies and there is an issue and it's a choice between delivering the girls or my wife's life, I already told them it will be my wife. It's morbid, I know, if the girls pass, then they will be left where they are until my wife is healthy enough to get them out. I instructed OB and the ICU to communicate with each other so that once Dallas is out of danger, we can revisit this conversation. She may not like the decision I have made, but I can't lose her and that's all there is to it.

December 23rd, Dallas is still on the ventilator, they are looking to remove it at the end of this week or beginning of next. They have decreased her meds again, so I am gearing up for her mood. I was correct; she is pissed today. She wanted me to take her out of the bed, they don't want to increase the meds again, so we just have to work through her coming back. I calmed her down finally and then helped with PT, she did about 15 minutes and then we got her back to bed. I brushed her hair and she seemed happy and then fell asleep. I tried to leave when she had fallen asleep. I need her to stay asleep so she will hopefully be calmer when she wakes. If I am there when she wakes up, she typically gets really agitated. I know this is only because she is confused and thinks I am there to take her home and when she realizes where she still is, she gets very upset.

Tonight, I am sitting outside by the fire with my kids Christa and Joey. Joey is Christa's brother who has moved in the barn to help me with my ranch, he feeds the animals and takes care of the outside, one less thing I have to worry about.

I feel like I have nothing to say when Dallas isn't here, I have nothing I want to talk about. No one, I want to talk too, it makes me genuinely see my life and my life with Dallas; it puts everything into perspective for me. I need my wife back.

December 24th, it is Christmas eve. I called the hospital for an update at 5 am, they said that Dallas had another good night of rest. She requested to brush her teeth multiple times per day, she's the only woman I know with the cleanest yet dirtiest mouth. The nurse told me they are still trying to get her off the ventilator, hoping there are no hiccups that stop this. As well as emailing her every day, I also took pictures and videos of everyday activities, mostly just me and Utley tooling around the house. Utley eating breakfast, Utley following dad around the yard; anything that will show her while she has been out for the last month, we have kept an even keel. I want Dallas to see when she comes back that I did everything I could for our daughter and that I made this horrible time the best for her that I could.

Let's Go
Chapter 15

December 24th, Best Christmas present ever. The ventilator has been removed.

December 25th, it is Christmas morning, and I called the hospital for the usual update. Last night when I left her, she was at 90% oxygen, during the night, they moved her to 75% then down to 50%, she is hanging strong at 50% oxygen with no ventilator and no ECMO machine. It truly is a miracle, not 10 days ago, the doctors weren't certain she and the babies would make it through the night. They were preparing me for the worse, I was wondering how I say goodbye to my girls, how I go on without them. Now she is battling her way back.

The twins seem to be unaffected, which is insane to me, with everything Dallas has been through those girls are still going strong. An ultrasound was done at 11 pm last night and the girl's heartbeats were 160 and 167, respectively.

I spent Christmas morning with my kids. I am a bit of a fish out of water being on my own. I want it to be special for them though, my boys are with me, and Utley and we open presents and have some breakfast. Utley loves it, she loves to open gifts, having a little one around always makes Christmas that much more fun. I head to the hospital later in the morning to spend the rest of the day with Dallas. I took some videos of Utley opening her presents to show her to put a smile on her face.

I'm feeling a little down today; I know I shouldn't be things are getting better, it's Christmas and she is getting better. I guess it's just the whole holiday situation, I want her to be at home. I want her to open gifts, watch Utley open her gifts and have dinner with us, it's so unfair that this has happened. I know once I see her face, I will feel better. But right now, I am feeling a little miserable.

December 26th, it's crazy to see my wife without all the tubes and lines all over her, and she is awake. The delirium is taking a toll on her, she says the strangest things; she said a man was sitting in the corner of her room, then there was a dog in the corner. The doctors say this is normal, but she has really lost a grip on reality and it's hard to digest. I try to see some humor in it but it's also strange to hear her talk like this. She really believes there is someone in her room. I humor her and tell her I see it too, so she doesn't get upset. You can't argue with someone that is coming out of sedation. I try not to read anything more into it, the doctors keep saying this too shall pass.

This morning besides the delirium being a little out of control. Dallas decided to pull her feeding tube out of her nose last night. She wants everything out and I get it, she is ready to go, but she is still not where we need her to be. I have spent the majority of the morning with her once again trying to keep her calm, she vomited as I was leaving, the nurses cleaned her up and got her settled again, her oxygen is at 40%, so it's coming down and that's a good thing. I was being asked a lot of questions, what day it was, did she miss Christmas, that was a hard one, yes you missed Christmas and the entire month of December. I think the delirium is starting to dissipate. They lowered her pain meds again, and she seems to be more comfortable and coherent.

December 27th, Oxygen is down to 30% and she is saying she is not in pain, trying to communicate with me more, writing sentences to me, but she still isn't making much sense.

December 28th, it's like I was on a roller coaster the last few days, she's off the ventilator and she is breathing on her own. However, she is still so confused, so as I am ecstatic that she is breathing on her own and the ventilator is gone, but she is out of it. It's hard to deal with, she called me yesterday so upset because she said the nurses left her in the hallway and I needed to come right away. I jumped in the car and sped down to the hospital, expecting her to be out in the hallway alone and scared. She was in her room and safely in bed. She yelled at me to leave again, so I left and like always, I came right back and she's fine and happy to see me again.

Last night she pulled out all her lines and decided she was going to stand up and leave the hospital and they had to restrain her. It is hard to see her tied down to a bed. I know this is temporary, but how temporary? Will she be normal after this, will she be the same woman I married? No one knows and no one can reassure me about anything, I just have to wait, and I am so tired of waiting. The nurses and doctors do their best to smile and let me know this is all part of the process, but I've never been through this before, I have never had to watch someone I love like this and it really freaks me out.

December 30th, I was with her again this morning and she told me that Utley, our two-year-old, stayed the night with her. Yesterday she was mad because I would not bring Utley to see her. I did the usual and asked her how that was and if she enjoyed it. I told her I could not bring Utley because she has school, but hopefully, I can get her to visit soon. The things she says to me make very little sense. So, I just have learned to roll with it. When it first started, I would argue with her and tell her.

"No Dallas, there is no one here."

"Utley didn't spend the night with you. "

It confused me, and I thought she was being serious; I didn't really correlate the drugs controlling her thoughts. Now I don't bother to correct or argue with her; I know she won't remember saying it anyways. I just go along with it and let her believe it.

I took her for a stroll in the wheelchair; we walked to the rose garden. I'm trying to spark something in her to let me know she's still in there. She's been really distant with me, I know it's the meds, at least I hope it's the meds, but it's still hard to take, I have no idea what's going through her head, and she's not telling me. I don't even think she knows.

I need to keep trying. The more I push, the more I know she will come back. I remind her of everything, the house, the animals, when we got married, when we met, Utley, the boys, anything to jog her memory a little bit. I talk to her about the future, the babies, how exciting it will be when they are finally home. We don't talk about what she went through in the last few months, I don't think she can fully comprehend what she has been through; I don't even know where to begin to start talking to her about it, I don't know what to ask, I know she doesn't remember for the most part and honestly that has to be so frustrating for her, to have a whole month of your life gone.

We have decided to move her to Peter's tower across the street, it is a rehab facility, it's still close to her team here and she will be able to get the physical and occupational therapy she needs. She has been immobile for over a month now and she gets tired quickly, hard to watch someone who ran marathons, lift weights and work out daily, now having to try to catch her breath just getting out of the chair. I am confident that once the girls are born and she gets the help she needs, she will be back to her old ways. It's a marathon, not a sprint, I continually remind myself.

I bought Dallas an iPad so she can start to correspond with people again. It will be good for her to see her friends and family and talk to them again. To fill them in on what's been going on, rather than always hearing it from me, I am still sending emails to her. However, I have stopped sending them to everyone else, a few people still hit me up to ask and I reply. Still, the amount who were calling and texting in the beginning to now has changed a lot. It says a lot about people, the ones that are still asking are the ones I know will still be around when this is all over.

I must say I miss talking to her the most; I don't have anyone that I can talk to, really talk to, this woman is my best friend, we go through life together we talk about everything and to be going through this makes me realize just how badly I want her to get better, how badly I need her in my life and how hard this has been to watch the love of my life go through this. Everyone has their ups and downs, but we always are together in what we do. I need that back. I need my wife back.

Today was rough, we laid Walt to rest. As much as I am so grateful that Dallas is pulling through. It kills me to know that they were both in the same situation, just down the hall from one another; this could have been me, burying my wife and children. I miss him, he was always so good to me, we both love classic cars and we talked about our upcoming car projects all the time. He would come to the office a few days a week and we would always chat. It's so hard to believe he's gone and it happened so fast, there was nothing wrong with him, which makes it so much worse, he had no underlying illness, that would make COVID that much worse, he was a healthy guy. None of it makes sense.

I have organized all the company vehicles to ride in procession behind the hearse. It's quite a sight, seeing 51 company vehicles all driving with their flashers on to the cemetery, Walt deserves more than this, he started this company, but with COVID, they won't let us all attend. 15 people and that's it, it sickens me to know that a man loved by so many is only allowed 15 people standing by his grave to pay respects. We can't even stand next to one another. We are all spread out over the cemetery. I lead the company trucks in procession around the graveyard as many times as possible before the staff tells me there are too many of us here and we have to leave. I tell everyone to make their way back out and stay and be with Mark and his family. The crazy part is, I have not told Dallas that Walt died, I don't know how either, and I don't know that she will even understand.

With Dallas still sick and Walt's death, I find myself being very angry inside. I don't like this feeling, usually I have an outlet where I work. I do things around the yard, but lately I'm just complacent and I don't know what to do. Nothing really makes me happy right now. I did decide to start walking and working out again; when I exercise, I feel better mentally, and I am hoping that will be a great outlet for me to decompress. I need an outlet and right now, I have nothing but my thoughts. I need to get out of my own head.

December 31st, It's just me, Christa, Joey, Maz (Christa's son), Evan and his girlfriend and of course Utley, it's New Year's Eve, what a change from last year. I ordered prime rib for everyone because I don't know how long I will be at the hospital and I don't feel like cooking a big meal tonight. After I get back from the hospital, it's a pretty quiet evening; the boys have friends over in the barn, so I am watching Jeopardy and chilling with Utley. I really want 2020 to end, but I don't want 2021 to start until Dallas is well. I hope the new year will bring a healthy wife and two beautiful baby girls' home to me. I want to put 2020 so far behind us.

Two Steps Forward, Three Steps Back
Chapter 16

January 1st, it's 2021, who would have thought my New Year's Day would have been spent in a hospital room, but here I am. Dallas doesn't want to eat, so I give her options: eat or stick a tube up her nose; she gave up rather quickly on this one.

I have noticed her heart rate has been elevated, I ask the doctors about it and they are going to run an EKG to be safe. They assure me it's probably her meds, but it's better safe than sorry. She is off all oxygen and breathing on her own, which I am sure is causing anxiety, which could explain the elevated heart rate. They also think it could be her thyroid, so they are running more tests. I am taking no chances.

January 2nd, something is wrong, I can feel it. This is not just delirium; she should have come out of this by now. I have expressed my concern to the doctors, and they have agreed to do an MRI scan. I wait patiently while they take her for yet another procedure. I have no idea what they could find, but I can feel in my bones that this is not coming out of sedation. Her eye is bloodshot like crazy and she is still angry and despondent. She has been through so much and I have read and been told that because of being on blood thinners with the ECMO, it can cause bleeding in the brain, I am praying this is not the case.

Four hours later and the MRI results are back, Dallas has a brain bleed on the right side of her brain, so in layman terms, she has had a stroke. They bring in the neuro team, she will be monitored closely, but due to being on ECMO and blood thinners, this is actually a common event. The positive part is that it has not affected her motor skills, but it explains her thoughts, anger and constant mood swings.

So, we will wait for the blood vessel to mend itself and if that doesn't happen, they will have to perform surgery to stop the bleeding. Just when I thought we were out of the woods, we are right back in it; I can't catch a break, this thing just keeps giving. But I am so glad they saw it and that my instinct was right.

The transfer to Peters Tower will have to wait, she is now in Neuro ICU. I have called the hospital and got an update that she is resting and comfortable. She is angry, but that can't be helped, we have another issue to deal with.

I was thinking back to the beginning of all of this and it's crazy because she tested positive for COVID once back in November, but never again and I find that surprising. Especially in a hospital setting where COVID is running rampant, I thought she would have gotten it again, but she hasn't; they have tested her multiple times, and all came back negative. It's so unpredictable, how can a healthy woman who is only 39 years old, get so sick. COVID, pneumonia and now a stroke. It baffles me that this is happening to her.

January 3rd, she is in room 1020, that shouldn't matter, should it? Not too many people would give a crap about the room number, but I do, I do not like even numbers; they are not good in my book, never have been good. When I was 21 years old, I went to Vegas for the first time. I bet one hundred dollars and I turned it into five grand, all the numbers ended in seven, is it superstition …. Maybe, do I believe in luck? I don't know but I live by these numbers 7,21; they hold some meaning to me and Dallas being sick and, in the hospital, doesn't change that. Had they transferred her to 1021, I would have been ok with it, but 1020? I'm not happy about this. I can't dwell on it though; I have bigger fish to fry right now. I have asked them to move her to another room, but nothing is available. I know it's crazy, but this is me, this is what goes through my mind. I have to get through this, no matter what room number she is in, I have no control over this and it's killing me.

Just before Dallas got sick, I bought a 2020 Dodge truck, it was a nice black truck and I had my work logo on its side, all the other employees got white ones and I got black. Then Dallas got sick, So, I gave the truck back, crazy, right? It was a feeling I had; the truck was bad luck. Once I had the truck, things started going bad for us, so I just got rid of it. So many people asked me.

"Hogi, what happened to your truck? "

I say.

"It was bad luck, so I sold it."

They think I'm kidding. They laugh and walk away and I am 100% serious. I sold it so quickly and went back to my 2019 Escalade. I bought my wife a 2020 G wagon, the same thing sold it back, it was the numbers. It just held bad feelings, everything started going downhill once I bought it and I didn't want anything around me that I didn't feel was right, so I got a white 2021 G wagon for her instead. 2021 made more sense to me. In my mind, it's a simple process. Not too many would understand, but I don't care, it's the way I am. Whether it's family members, material items, furniture, animals, books, friends, it does not matter, if it has any type of negative connotation, then I will get rid of it. Life is too short of having negative energy and this situation has solidified that for me.

Time To Heal

Chapter 17

Jan.4th, the Neuro team has said she is progressing, the bleeding has stopped on its own and the body has absorbed the blood, they will perform another MRI in two weeks to make sure nothing new has started and the bleed has healed completely. Her motor skills and speech were not affected; however, it has affected her attitude and mood, she is irritable, emotionless and just an all-around ass right now; I again have to remember this is the illness and not her, but it's tough right now. When she yells at me to leave one minute and then the next ask why I wasn't here, it's a lesson in patience and I feel I have had my fill of being patient and understanding. It's an emotional rollercoaster.

No one has said,

'Hey Hogi, how are you doing through all this? How are you dealing with it?"

"Anything we can do to help?"

No, it's always

"How is Dallas? How are the twins."

"We are praying."

I totally get it, I understand completely, I am not sick, I was not the one who has been in the hospital for the last month and a half. But I feel that people tend to forget that the family members are the one that remembers it all, watching your loved one go through all of it, seeing them unconscious and so ill. Dallas thankfully will not remember the majority of this and for that grateful.
However, I still have to live with this, seeing my wife completely incapacitated, living every day asking is this the day I become a single dad, is my daughter going to see her mom again. It is a lot to take, I think once you're near the end, you go through a type of PTSD about it all, because when it's happening, you have no time, there is no time to wallow in self-pity and lay in your bed and cry. Your adrenaline is keeping you going, and you don't slow down for anything if you do it could all come crashing down. The minute my mind stops is when I start obsessing over it, how it happened,

why it happened and what I could have done to prevent it.

A lot of men would not be able to handle this, they would have folded, this is not for the weak and I am not patting myself on the back by any means. The easiest thing to have done would have been to fold and leave it all behind me. That's not who I am. I adhered to my vows, for better for worse, through sickness and health. I didn't ask for this and I know she sure as hell didn't, but I wasn't giving up now. You don't walk away, this is a fight, you get up every day and you approach it with positivity and strength, this could have gone another way, it still could, it's not over, but I'm not going anywhere, we will always be together in this. I can say without a doubt I would not wish this on my worst enemy.

January 5th, the OB docs were concerned about one of the girls today, so they are doing high-end ultrasounds daily, they made us sign consents so if they see a problem that they can go in and get the girls out via C section. We both have to sign and both be in agreement with this. Dallas is not eating much, her appetite isn't there, but for her sake and the girls, she needs to keep going. Once again, I have to hammer away because the docs said if she isn't going to eat, she goes back on the feeding tube. She doesn't want this, more tubes are not what she wants, so I have to keep encouraging her to eat.

I went to Peter's tower today to make sure everything was good, they are ready for her.

Hopefully, in the next few days, she will be cleared out of Neuro ICU and we can get her settled in at Peters and start the rehab process. The doctors tell me she could be there for months. I am gearing up for this. It's already been almost two months. My days are pretty routine now, I am used to the constant back and forth. I even joked that I was going to have my mail forwarded here to the hospital since it's where I spend most of my time. I have a cool little hideout outside the electrical room, it's outdoors and quiet and I can just go and chill over there and drown out everything in my head. It's where I go when things get too much for me. I won't be sad, though, if I never have to come back to this hospital.

January 6th today was a better day. Dallas was more proactive, I am hoping that when she recovers and reads all my emails and this book, she will see what I went through; I never want to diminish what she went through, this was all her and I know it, this is just a different side, the helpless feeling every day, the praying to God to give her sickness to me, never knowing what I would wake to? Dreading the phone ringing just in case it was bad news. Now that she is more alert and awake, I am trying desperately to get her back. I still do not know what the repercussions of the stroke are, as of now, her short-term memory is short, she will tell me something and then a few minutes later tell me again. The doctors say this is normal and part of the process, but when you have never experienced something like this, it is anything but normal.

Neuro has some strict rules about electronics, making sense that the lights and all the flickering can cause brain issues in patients in the neurological ward. So the iPad I bought for Dallas is only programmed for my kids, her best friend Christa and my mom and me. I do not want her to get overwhelmed. She can only have it for short periods of time and I know if everyone has access, they won't leave her alone, I have to be selective with who she speaks with, and some people won't like that. There are people that care and I know who they are, but some just want to know what's going on, they want to gossip and tell others what they think they know. To get through this, she needs to rest and have her brain rest, and to do that, she needs zero distractions.

The New Normal
Chapter 18

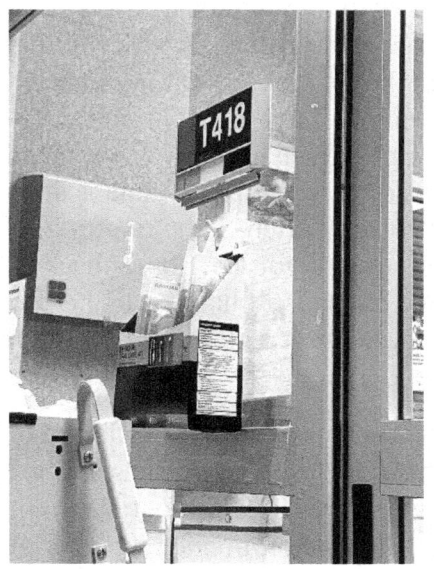

January 10th, I brought IN and OUT for all the hospital staff on the ward today, they all seemed happy about that. OB docs came in and were shocked at how well things are going and how well the babies are. I convinced the nursing staff to let me stay the night tonight; we watched a football game together and had dinner. I went downstairs and got her a smoothie for dessert; it was the best night I have had in a long time. I fell asleep in the chair next to the bed and got to wake up next to her in the morning. It was indeed a perfect Sunday evening.

January 11th, I headed home to see my little one and I decided to take her to work with me for a bit before school. Utley and I have spent so much time together, just her and I; she is a bundle of energy and every time I look at her, I see Dallas. She truly keeps me going. Some days I just wanted to throw in the towel, I look at my little girl and I am reminded of what I am fighting for. I wish I could bring her to see her mama, we spend all day talking about her, she thinks mama is at a resort right now getting better. Some mornings she wakes up and goes to look for her, comes back to get me, and tells me mama isn't home. I let her know mama will be home soon. It's all I think about; getting my wife home.

Today she was being transferred to Peters Tower. That place is legit. She has all the best people to work with her and continue to motivate her. Lynn, the director, bonded with her quickly. I was happy because this situation can be extremely hard and frustrating. Hence, she needs someone in her corner beside me that can get her spirits up and keep them up. I cannot be here 24/7, so when I am not here, I need to know she is in the best hands, I need her to be motivated whether I am here or not.

She is now in a new room at Peter's on the 6th floor; to this day she has been in 6 different rooms, 4 different buildings. It's crazy now, to look back and think that ten days ago life was completely different as much as I have tried to stay positive, it has been a complete and utter rollercoaster of a ride. My emotions have been all over the place. I have been angry, happy, sad, lonely, distraught. I have tried very hard not to show it or take it out on anyone, I know there are a few people at work that got the short end of the stick when it comes to my attitude. They know what I am going through and who I am, so I know they won't hold it against me. That being said, my personal struggle is no excuse to be an ass to people either, so I tried to keep a level and calm head for the most part, but sometimes it just was not happening.

January 12th, Dallas woke up in her new room with me sitting next to her. I stayed for the whole day, she is having two workouts per day, so I stayed to help and cheer her on. Thursdays are bid days at my office, so I like to see what is coming through, so I was back and forth. I am spending more time at work and catching up on a lot that I have missed. I did my best to stay in touch with everyone, but when you are going through a crisis like this, work is not always at the forefront of my mind. I did take Utley to a lot of jobs, she would drive around with me to open job sites and to check on the crew. It was nice having her with me; she's my little sidekick. I had a big project over at a company called Valley Wide beverage, I have become tight with the owner and his family. They always ask how Dallas is doing and they asked me to bring her by so they could meet her when all of this is done. It's crazy that I still got the project done in time before the new year through all the personal matters I was dealing with. I think staying busy helped me a lot and got me through a lot of this, it would take my mind off what was happening at the hospital. I took Utley there a few times when I was checking on things, she likes seeing the job sites, and at least she and I get to be together.

Dallas is starting to get restless; she really wants to come home. I can see her anxiety level is high; with everything she has been through and still has to go through, I can understand why, I try my best to let her know that it doesn't matter, none of it matters, we will get through it together. Like we always do. But she has doubts and misgivings and I understand that we don't know what lies ahead, we just have to keep on going.

January 13th, today another ultrasound was performed, Dallas decided to change OB's today and that made me immensely happy. It was time for a change, we needed a doctor that was there for her, and we both agreed to making a change. I thought that the original doctor who told me to keep her home didn't really understand how sick she was and didn't really care. I wanted Dallas to make the decision, though, because she is the one having the babies and she is the one who needs to be comfortable with her doctor, when it comes to giving birth. I'm just there to be supportive and be the dad, she's the one doing all the work. I think now knowing everything she went through and the fact that the doctor wanted her to stay home and told us she was not that sick has made her rethink it all.

I surprised my kids this afternoon. I didn't want to tell them in case it didn't happen so, around 2PM I told them all to meet me at the house, we were going to see Dallas. All of us. It is the first time anyone but me has been allowed up. I was excited for them, especially Utley; she didn't deserve any of this, she's so young and sweet and she missed her mom so much. I also wanted to see the look on my Dallas' face when she sees her again. We all head up there, the boys and their girlfriends and Utley and I. It's a bittersweet moment for me to watch my daughter run up to her mom and hug her, I get chills just thinking about it, it's all I hoped for these last two months, to see everyone together again as a family. The kids loved it, we took a group photo, we all wore masks to keep her safe. We didn't overstay because she was so tired and I didn't want her to get overwhelmed and exhausted. When we got home, Utley fell asleep so quickly, all the excitement of seeing her mom wore her out. She was so happy so I just let her sleep on me and held her tight.

It's January 14th, I am back and forth, as usual it's a lot nicer to know I am coming to the hospital to talk to her, that she knows I am there and can converse with me. It was so hard before, every day walking into the unknown; first she was unconscious and then she was just angry, now that the bleeding is starting to heal you can see the shift in her personality, it's like she likes me again. She still has a lot of anxiety about the future, and I get that. It's pretty scary not knowing if this could happen again, or if she is more susceptible to strokes now, her lungs? Are they healed or is there going to be irreversible damage from being on a ventilator and ECMO? These are all questions I, too have asked myself, and we don't know, we don't know what the future holds, all I know is that we are in it together and after getting through this, there is nothing we can't do. The doctors are optimistic and cautious, we have to keep an eye on her and make sure she doesn't get sick again, but in the end she's alive and with me so it's all good.

January 15th, I went in early today, I wanted to sit and watch her, just watch her sleep and be peaceful and breathe, breathe on her own no machines, no bells and alarms. Just my wife, her chest rising and falling with her own breaths. It's these little things in life that you take for granted. Watching someone breathe, you never know when you won't get to see that again, so this morning I got a coffee and a bagel, and I sat and waited for her to wake up. She finally wakes about 6:15 am and she sees I am there and smiles if she only knew how many times I have wished for this day. She gets going and starts her workouts; she is getting a few in a day, so it makes her very tired. I usually wait until she has dozed off before I leave again and then come back later in the afternoon. Today I rushed back home to grab Utley. She loves school, So I am trying to get back home to be able to drop her off and then I go back to get her around 2:30. I like to spend a few hours with her before I head back out to the hospital. Tonight, I am taking everyone for dinner, I hope it will be the last dinner I will have without Dallas with me.

January 16th, I woke up so late this morning, this is how you know things are better, for the last month and a half I have been sleeping in two-hour increments, I fall asleep, then I wake up with a start, surprised I even fell asleep, then my mind starts, and I can't get back to sleep. But last night I slept from 6:30 pm to 6:30 am. I needed it. Even though Utley slept in, she needed it too. She and I get going and Christa is here to take her to school so I can get to the hospital.

I spent the day there, they took Dallas to PT, so I jumped in her bed to wait for her and I fell asleep; I don't even know how, those beds are so uncomfortable, but I was passed out. When I woke, the roles were reversed and she was sitting next to the bed watching me, it was cool to wake up too. We took a walk around the hospital grounds; it was a nice treat to get her out of her room and just walk around together. It exhausted her, so when we got back, I watched golf and she slept. I decided to spend the night at the hospital.

Home

Chapter 19

January 17th, I came home from the overnight stay at the hospital and showered, Utley had just gotten up, so I decided to take her across the street to the church. She loves it there, loves the singing. It's peaceful, I don't go often. I am not every Sunday type of guy. Today felt different, I had a lot to be thankful for, so I decided to go. We got back home at 11 and I got ready to head back to the hospital.

I got up to the hospital and I was absolutely floored, they told me Dallas could go home. I could not believe it, she has only been at Peter's for less than a week, I was told she could be there for months, maybe even up until the babies are born. I did not anticipate this at all. I am excited and ready, but completely shocked. Dallas is ecstatic of course she wants to come home, and I know she's also nervous, everything has changed yet everything is the same, if that makes any sense at all. She's missed out on so much and still has to stay healthy and have the babies. it's not over, it's not like she gets to come home, and we just go about the days, there is physical therapy, MRI's, X-rays, fetal monitoring, everything that was right there at our fingertips will be a little less accessible, it just means I have to take her to these appointments. The doctors say twice a week for the ultrasounds. With physical therapy we can have someone come to the house. Christa is still here, so she will be able to help since I have to work still. I don't want her to be alone in the house, so Christa has agreed to stay on and help with Utley and the new babies until we know Dallas is completely out of the woods. I don't want to deal with any of this now, all I think about is that she is coming home.

January 18th, I get to the hospital and the director Lynn is prepping Dallas to go home. She informs her that there are news reporters' downstairs and they all want to interview her. First in the room, there will be pictures and questions; then when we head down to the lobby, there will be another crew waiting for pictures and interviews. I am not too sure how this came about or who informed the local media about it, but it is a hot topic. In California, there has never been a woman pregnant with twins who had COVID, contracted pneumonia, was on a ventilator and an ECMO machine and lived to speak about it. Of course, people wanted to know what was happening. I am not comfortable with these things, so it's all her, it's her story to tell.

They started at the beginning and how she thought she had a bad cold and how it progressed. She explained how in early December she couldn't take it anymore and told the nurses to ventilate her. They were lapping it up; Fresno/Clovis is a small area of California and for this to have happened in our small town was big news. It was all over the TV, ABC30, Med watch, she sat in the hospital bed and gave her story.

They interviewed Doctor Ives as well, and some of the nurses. When it was time to go downstairs, I got her into her wheelchair and went out the front hospital doors. Then we saw the reporters and TV crews, its then that I knew this was a big time. I didn't say a word and let Dallas tell her story, I stood stoically and quietly behind her like a bodyguard; they asked what her biggest fear was, and she stated it was losing the babies. She told them honestly, she never went in thinking she could die, it didn't cross her mind. She also gave some advice, in which you have to listen to your body because had she not, we wouldn't be here today.

I get Dallas in the car, and we say our goodbyes to everyone, we thank them, and we hug them, and it is a bittersweet moment to finally be leaving this place. We make the trek home; the kids are all there waiting for us as well as Christa. I am not too sure what to expect from Dallas right now, so much has happened. I have so much to catch up on, but I have no idea where to start, I don't know how much she remembers. Does she remember that Walt died, or that I closed her law firm? Will she like her new car and the acre of grass I planted with a new playset for the girls?

I sold our Pismo beach house while she was in the hospital. Will she remember that we put it on the market before she got sick? I still have to schedule movers to get all our stuff out, I haven't talked to her about any of this yet. I guess right now I should relish that I have my family back together, everything else can wait.

Day To Day
Chapter 20

So far, having Dallas home is wonderful, but it isn't without challenges. I notice she has a lot of anxiety; she is very worried about what is to come. I try to reassure her that everything will be ok, but I also understand the anxiety, she almost died. She has a giant gap in which she doesn't remember anything that happened for a month. I can't begin to imagine what this was like for her, I just need to be patient and help her get through this the best I know how.

Everyone wants to come to visit and see her, but I am keeping everyone away for now, it's too much for her and she will get overwhelmed, for now it's just her and I and the kids. COVID has only gotten worse, and I cannot take the chance that she could get it again, no one even knows if you can get it twice. She got vaccinated against it, but who knows what type of protection that will afford her. There is too much uncertainty still and not enough research on the vaccine itself, and I'm not taking any chances. I think it's a miracle that she is alive, and home and I intend on keeping it that way.

It's only January and the babies are not due until the end of April, so I need to ensure she stays healthy. She is not out of the woods. Everyone is under the impression that since the hospital released her everything is good and she's 100%. Yes, it's great. She's home, she is with me, but she is by no means out of the woods. I am hypervigilant about everything at this point, after everything we just went through, I am not taking any chances.

She still has to do lots of testing, I take her back to Community Regional Medical Center 3-4 times a week for fetal nonstress tests, they attach a belt to Dallas abdomen to measure both babies heartbeats. This seems a bit much, but with everything that she has gone through and the fact that the twins can come early, they need to check on them frequently. This along with checking her lungs and heart rate and making sure she is feeling good. It's not ideal, but we do what we must in order to ensure healthy babies and a healthy mom. Everything so far is good; this is what the doctors are telling us. The only issue now is that one of the babies is in breech position, so they have decided that they will schedule Dallas for a C-section, they are saying the end of April, but of course, that could change so we wait and go to our weekly Non stress tests.

January 19th, she's home. I slept beside my wife last night. It's a bit surreal not to have to wake up alone and head to the hospital. I wake up constantly to check on her though. Her breathing is still labored and that is to be expected for being on the ventilator for so long. Her energy is down as well, she is only getting bigger with the twins, so she is napping a lot and getting tired easily. We have to discuss whether she can start driving again, but that is not at the forefront right now.

She has had to adjust to the changes I have made, nothing big but just cleaning and organizing and moving things around. Her memory is still not great, she repeats herself 3-5 times. Sometimes forgets what I told her in the morning, when I get to work; she will call me and not remember what we already discussed. It's a lesson in patience for me. But I know that the brain can heal itself and it takes time, so I have hope and remain patient and understanding with her.

Dallas wants to do something nice for the hospital, mainly the patients; we were lucky because I was able to see her. Not many patients get that luxury right now. When I wasn't able to go to the hospital, we depended on facetime to talk to one another. So, we decided to donate iPad to the ICU patients and their families. This is just a way to give back to the community and thank everyone for their support. As well as helping others who are not fortunate to have access to the hospital during this horrific time. The hardest part of your loved one being sick and in the hospital is not being able to see them. With iPads, we were able to see Dallas, we could correspond with her nurses, and she could see the kids. Dallas could see what was going on at home, it was nice to have some sort of communication. Even through a screen.

So, we met with the Community Regional Medical Center Foundation Director who was more than happy to help us out. We had a truck deliver the iPads and Dallas and Utley gave them out. It was a pleasant experience to give back, not everyone can afford to have a tablet or phone or iPad, so it's something that we can do to help and since we just went through it, we understand why it's so important. It was received very well and again; the newspapers and TV stations came out to take pictures and talk to Dallas. I stood by and watched. I was so proud of Dallas for everything she has been through, and now giving to others, it's so selfless. Most people would be at home keeping to themselves and healing, but not my wife, she and Utley are handing out iPads like its Christmas morning.

Dallas is now adjusting to being a stay-at-home mom. I, too, am adjusting to having a stay-at-home wife. Since the minute we met, she has been on the go all the time, work, the ranch, Utley. This will be an adjustment for everyone, especially her, she will probably be busier than ever, having three girls under the age of three. Nevertheless, having to walk away from a decade long career is not something that she will take lightly, I am not taking it lightly; this is huge, to not be able to go back to what you love, it's not just the month she missed, the scariness of the situation she was in, now it's the end of her career. No one considers the consequences of this whole thing, it's just the constant questions.

"Is she home?"

"Is she good?"

I always answer with, "Yes she's home."

"Everything is good."

But really no one has any idea of any of it, and I can't even begin to put into words what it was like. Her life has completely changed and it's another situation we have to get through.

The future is scary, that's the truth, we never expected any of this and now we have to hope and pray that everything will be ok moving forward.

I have a couple of guys from my office go over to her law office to help her clean things out. I waited for her to be well enough to do this. It's going to be emotional for her, knowing this is it. It's her career and it is her office; it wasn't for me to take all her stuff and throw it into the back of a truck and be done with it. This is closure for her, and she needs it. She, Christa and Utley head over and start going through everything. I leave her to it; she doesn't need my help in this.

At home, she is nesting, getting the nursery ready for the girls; in between napping and physical therapy, she is doing better but we still have a long road ahead. We take off to the coast a few times over the next few weeks just to get away, get out of Clovis. We need time away, walks on the beach. The kids come with us and we are all back together as a family. I try to give Dallas her space, she does not need me hovering, but I worry about her being on her own. I go to work as usual and come home for lunch, I make sure she is all good before heading back out again. Christa is here with her, so I have peace of mind that she isn't alone. Things are slowly going back to normal. We are still careful about who comes over, we have not been very social since she came home, we don't want to expose her to anything unnecessarily. I am cautious of who I am with at work and who I see socially. So, we spend our time together as a family and we make the best of it.

Once again, this is the new normal, it's better than what I was doing before but nonetheless it's a lot. The non-stress tests for the babies keep us busy. Back and forth to the hospital. I really thought once I got her home, we would be home for good. But with the babies' tests and the MRI's and the brain scans for her, we are at the hospital just as much. They want to keep an eye on the babies, and I get It, I am grateful but it's exhausting. Her due date is the end of April, but they are saying it could be anytime. But at this point, one little issue and she is far enough along to take the babies. The days seem to drag now, when you're waiting for something like this, it can seem like forever. Normal pregnancies are hard but her whole pregnancy seems like it was the longest nine months of my life.

They started steroid shots for the girls' lungs, if they need to take them, then we at least want their lungs to be strong.

We are now at the end of March, and she has been home for two months. It has been awesome, but also an adjustment. We let go of our nanny, Christa is still living with us and has taken over all the nanny duties. Utley is still going to preschool every day and she loves it. She sings songs and is learning so much, it's great to see that this whole situation hasn't affected her. I am so grateful that she is so young and will hopefully never remember this.

Dallas is home and resting and getting ready. It's any day at this point. Last doctor's visit she was dilated to a 4. Still no contractions and one of the girls is still in breech position. So, we know the C-section will be the way to go. I don't want her to go into active labor, because then it will be an emergency C-section. I want this to go to plan, but I am fully aware that I have no control over any of it.

I've been thinking about all of this since it happened, and it is still surreal to me that only two months ago I almost lost everything. I have been questioning the "why"; why me, why her, why us. I have always tried to live my love in a giving way. I can't help but think I was being punished for something, the old saying of what doesn't kill you makes you stronger, resonates in my mind now. I almost broke. This almost broke me; I could have so easily folded, walked away, said, I am done or I can't, for some reason I was being tested, I was losing my girls and I can't fathom why. What did I do to deserve this? What did Dallas do? It shows you that no matter how good of a person you are, or how you try to live your life, there are going to be obstacles, obstacles that will test every fiber in your body. It will be something that will change the course of your life forever.

It's Time
Chapter 21

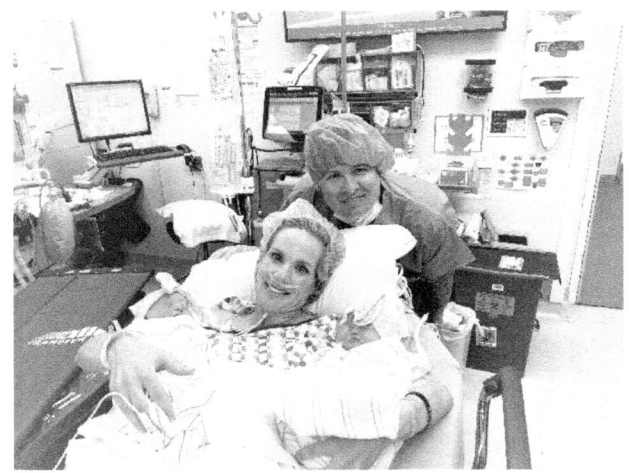

It is now the first week of April, Dallas is still dilated and it's getting close. The babies are doing good, but it's time. We get the call on April 6th to head to the hospital on the 7th; how insane is that 4/7/21. I couldn't have planned that any better. We have a 10 am check-in time. The morning of the 7th, I get up and go to work for a quick meeting and then head back to get Dallas, we are ready to go. Utley is with Christa, so we are good to go.

We get to the hospital, and they check us in; thankfully I am allowed to be with her the whole time, I don't have to call any hospital staff to plead my case. I head straight to the maternity wing with her and while they prep her, I sit and wait. It's finally here, my girls will be born today, so many days I thought this day would never come. I have for the last 4 months held my head high and preserved through the storm that has come barreling through my life. I am beyond grateful that this day is here, I'm nervous and excited and just want everything to go smoothly.

They get Dallas prepped, start her IV, get the monitoring going while waiting for the OR to call. It's now 11:15 am and we are anxious, it's all so real now. Two girls will be brought into the world today, we have had months of testing, so we know they are good, but there is always a bit of unknown until you see them and can hold them in your arms. Dallas was on a feeding tube for over a month, she lost so much weight and all those nutrients went to the babies, we don't know how much they will weigh; doctors say 4-5 lbs. each, that seems so small to me, but I am reassured by the nurses that that is not considered premature.

This is all new to me, all my kids thus far have been born naturally, so the C-section part is a little daunting, I'm not sure what to expect. I don't know how Dallas will fare through it all. They bring us into the OR, and they give Dallas a spinal; it's an epidural so she won't feel anything from the waist down, it's crazy, she can be awake while they cut her body open and take two children out of her. They drape a sheet just below her neckline, so we can't see anything. There are machines and monitors and sounds and smells that I don't like. As I stated many times before, I don't like hospitals. I have spent more time in one in the last year than I would have ever cared too. Today though, is different. It's a happy day. It's the day I get to meet my girls, it has been a long time coming and I am happy and anxious.

    4/7/21 12:52 pm Hayze Renee Selling makes her debut, she weighs 6lbs 10oz. and is 20" long

    Followed one minute later at 12:53 pm by Harvee Seven Selling at 5lbs 14oz. and 19.5" long

    They are here, my girls are here, and they are fine. They are crying and honestly, it's the best sound I've ever heard. Dallas is crying but these are happy tears. I'm in awe of all of this. How Dallas came through this sickness and kept my girls safe, how they are here now, and Dallas is here, and we can finally be complete. I cut the cords and the nurses swaddle them up and give them to us, they are so small; I am carrying these tiny little humans and I am in utter disbelief that the day has finally come. It's almost like a huge weight has just been lifted from my shoulders. I can breathe, and I can finally be free of all the worries that have plagued me these last six months; it was all for this day, my girls are all here and they are healthy, and they are beautiful.

How It Came to Be

Chapter 22

My story is done, the worst and best part of my life is over and I can look back and say I made it.

The idea of this book wasn't solely mine. After Dallas had come home out of the ICU, I had resumed life back to somewhat of a normal state. I was at the dentist's office and was sitting next to a lovely elderly lady, she said I looked familiar. She had asked if she knew me from somewhere and I replied that I didn't think so. Then it came to her.

"You were on TV."

"Wasn't your wife very sick"?

So, I reply,

"Oh yup, that was me."

So, she starts asking me all the questions,

"Is your wife good now?"

"Are your babies here"?

I replied with.

"Yes, she is home, and no, the babies aren't born yet".

We start talking and I tell her everything, this stranger I have never met before, but I pour my heart out to her and I tell her everything, things I haven't told even my closest friends.

When I am done, she said

"You should write a book."

I respond with,

"No chance"

She laughs and says, "You have a story here, this is real life and what happened to you and your family is a miracle."

I laughed it off, I thanked her for listening to me and we went our separate ways.

Once back in my car, I thought about what she said, realizing she was right. I do have a story here. This was sudden and intense, and no one saw it coming and we were thrown into this wild ride without knowing the outcome, not knowing what each day would bring. I had prepared myself at one point to say goodbye to my wife and my daughters. It is unthinkable, now to look back as I hold my baby girls, that they almost didn't make it. I think I have a bit of PTSD about the whole thing. Writing this book was so hard because I had to relive it every day, going through all those emotions reliving the trauma and the fear. I haven't talked to anyone about it. I probably should see someone. I am writing this book as a sort of therapy, to tell my story. When friends ask; how's it going, I just respond with the usual,

"It's good"

I don't know that anyone can really understand it, I don't even know if I truly understand it. I don't know what to say.

Some will question why I wrote this book, I was dead set against it at the beginning, when this lady mentioned it, I thought that is the craziest thing I have ever heard, why would I write a book about the hardest time of my life and who would even read it. I don't know how to write a book, and who do I ask? I ended up googling a lot of it and found a publisher that would help me. Luckily, I wrote everything down so I had it all to go back on as a reference and it was still very prevalent in my mind, you don't just walk away from these situations unscathed.

I am a private guy; I didn't really want the attention. Then I thought about it and realized this is not a sad story, this is a positive story. This is a story that anyone can relate to, young, old, sick, healthy. The news is full of sadness and despair. Look at all these people dying of COVID when do you ever see the other side. The side where, yes, someone has COVID. They are fighting for their life and the lives of their unborn children, and it has a positive outcome. It is so rare, and it needs to change, these stories of triumph and strength need to be told, people need to know that you can make it through this, and that death isn't always the outcome. This story is different, it's not written in the patient's voice, I don't want to take away from that, I want to tell a different perspective. It's not just about what Dallas went through, because she doesn't remember a lot of it. it's what we, her family went through. Not just the sick person and if she is going to pull through, and how she got through, but the family at home, how do they keep going, what does that look like? How do you keep your family at home healthy, safe and sane, as well as yourself and your sick wife and two unborn babies? It can happen and I am proof.

I was asked to write a foreword for this book. A thank you of sorts to all those that helped this book come to fruition. That was a hard part for me, because first off no one knew I was writing it. Not one person. Most people would thank friends and family and those that rallied beside you; But I thank myself, and yes, I know that sounds crazy, but in the end, after all is said and done, I got through this on my own. I didn't have anyone walking next to me holding my hand and telling me what to do, or how to handle the curveballs that were being thrown at me daily or what would come next. I had to rely on myself and find my own inner strength to go through the days and take care of myself and my children at home as well as my wife. It's not selfish, I just don't believe in giving other people accolades they don't deserve. Yes, people called me, yes, people brought me food and helped me with my daughter, but in the end, I was alone; I woke up alone, I went to sleep alone and I went through my days alone. So, in the end I want to thank myself for not giving up, for not walking away, for not breaking down, and for getting through the hardest 57 days of my life on my own.

Made in the USA
Las Vegas, NV
08 August 2021